DARFIELD & WOMBWELL:
A SECOND SELECTION

BRIAN ELLIOTT

SUTTON PUBLISHING

Sutton Publishing Limited
Phoenix Mill · Thrupp · Stroud
Gloucestershire · GL5 2BU

First published 2003

Title page photograph: cyclist David Biffen
pauses for the camera of his travelling
companion, Tom Gibson, at the Wombwell
boundary (Aldham Bridge, Wombwell
Lane), prior to embarking on an extensive
cycling and youth hostel holiday, 1966.
(*D. Biffen*)

British Library Cataloguing in Publication Data
A catalogue record for this book is available from the
British Library.

ISBN 0-7509-3039-X

Typeset in 10.5/13.5 Photina.
Typesetting and origination by
Sutton Publishing Limited.
Printed and bound in England by
J.H. Haynes & Co. Ltd, Sparkford.

An interesting Edwardian scene at Church Street, Darfield, *c.* 1905. The hackney coachman and his two
draught horses wait patiently for the photographer to take the photograph, as do several children, a young
man on the pavement and a telegraph boy, standing to attention outside the council offices. (*Old Barnsley*)

CONTENTS

A happy group of Low Valley children, probably getting ready for a chapel Whit Walk, superbly captured by the camera of Wombwell photographer R.J. Short in about 1948. (*G. Smallman/R.J. Short*)

Familiar shops and businesses advertised in the Darfield parish magazine for 1959.
(*Esther Johnson*)

INTRODUCTION

Welcome to *Darfield and Wombwell: a Second Selection*. Like its predecessor, this volume does not aim to be a definitive history, but it should provide present and future readers with useful glimpses and memories of an area that, in many respects, has changed almost beyond recognition over the last century. The assembly of this compilation has been completed in order to complement and enhance the previous publication. In this respect, I have included more than 230 photographs and images, the great majority of which have never been published before. A good number of these are from family albums and private collections, so I am immensely grateful to many individuals and organisations for the loan of material. Anyone researching and writing about twentieth-century Darfield and Wombwell can not help but come across the excellent work of a number of local photographers, particularly the professional work of R.J. ('Joe') Short (1903–81) who, over so many years, contributed so much to our local social history. I met Joe on one or two occasions, through his young assistant, David Biffen, and remember on one occasion 'having a go' at processing one of my films in his Barnsley Road studio. A few years ago I paid tribute to his work and other Barnsley area photographers in a supplement of the *Photohistorian*, published by the Royal Photographic Society. Captions to all the images are entirely my own and great care has been expended in obtaining as much accurate information as possible. However, and understandably, I have had to rely on personal memory and information from various individuals and families in order to facilitate this process. Identification of unnamed individuals and more information about particular places are most welcome. I would also appreciate any individual, business or organisation contacting me if they have photographs or ephemera relating to the locality. Such material could contribute to further publications.

The use of oral testimony has given a new dimension to this volume. I was able to interview and record the memories of about a dozen remarkable individuals. I am extremely grateful for their co-operation and kindness; and also for the support of their families. It has been a great privilege to be able to chat, for example, with Mrs Hilda Perrin, née Camplejohn, Barnsley's oldest resident, who could recall Queen Victoria and the coronation of Edward VII. It was also a marvellous experience to listen to the anecdotes of 102-year-old John Bailey and the considerable memories of Florence Copeland and her aunt, Mary Evans. Geoffrey Shone, Colin Leech, Malcolm Hambleton, the late Margaret Crawford and Malcolm Robinson have been extremely kind to provide both oral information and source material for the book. I am indebted to the kindness and help of Bill and Barbara Marsden and members of Low Valley Methodist Church. I am also grateful for exceptionally useful family history information and personal tributes from Betty Adams, Olwyn Beard, Lynn Bembridge, Dennis and Hazel Camplejohn, Zena Hudson, Esther and Martyn Johnson, Julie and Michael Little, Margaret Mann, Barbara Sanders and Terry Sykes.

Finally, I would like to thank Simon Fletcher, Michelle Tilling and all the staff at Sutton Publishing for their help and encouragement.

Young photographer's assistant David Biffen in Joe Short's studio, 64 Barnsley Road, Wombwell, 1964. (*David Biffen*)

1

Schooldays

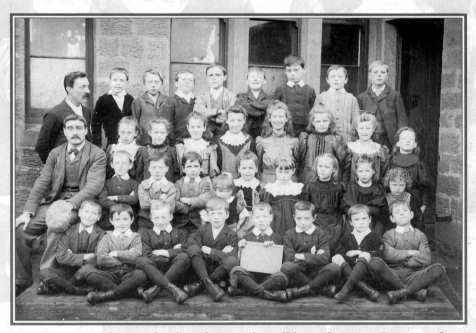

Thirty-two senior boys and girls and two male staff from Class A at Great Houghton School, *c.* 1905. The lads are wearing short, knee-length trousers, long socks and laced ankle boots; and several wear Norfolk jackets. The girls wear smart dresses. Dorothy Adams is fifth from the left (tallest girl) in the middle row of girls. These would be working-class and a few lower-middle-class children wearing their best clothes for a very special occasion: the visit of Holdsworth & Wilkinson (photographers) from Hepworth, near Huddersfield. (*Betty Adams*)

A large group of young children and their class teacher, Mrs Goodall, from Darfield Church School, *c.* 1919. Several of the boys (such as Norman Welford) wear sailor blouses or suits, and some of the girls wear ribbons in their hair. Other named children include Marjorie Rimmer, Victor Howdle and ? Cox. (*Betty Adams*)

Senior pupils at Low Valley School in 1949. Back row, left to right: Harry Croft, Roy Wolcott, David Griffiths, Billy Shaw (died in his teens), Ralph Connolly, Lawrence Smedley, John Gill, Billy Askin (died in his teens), Irving Ward, Bill Marsden and Mrs Roach (teacher). Third row: Alf Dunn, Fred Sullivan, Jack Foster, Peter Dawson, Jack Firth, Leslie Jinks, Leslie Powell, Harry Barnett and Donald Bird. Second row: Joyce Sayles, Ann Dyson, Agnes Lee, Pat Haller, Joyce ?, Sylvia Button, Rita Goodwin, Joyce Gaskin, Anne Dyson, Sylvia Gray. Front row: Tom Hazledene, Roy Barnet, Alan Herbert, Tom Williams, Ernest Wainwright and Colin Harper. Their future occupations include those of teacher, lecturer, nurse, engineer, care worker, policeman, joiner, driving instructor and Co-op manager. (*Bill Marsden*)

A standard letter from the Education Officer at County Hall (West Riding County Council) to the parents of Miss Esther Weigh, inviting her attendance at the new Wombwell Middle (Selective Senior) School, on Monday 8 April 1929. This was the precursor of Wombwell High School. (*Esther Johnson*)

29
Circular—E.
30

COUNTY COUNCIL OF THE WEST RIDING OF YORKSHIRE.
EDUCATION DEPARTMENT.

COUNTY HALL,
WAKEFIELD.
March, 1929.

WOMBWELL MIDDLE (Selective Senior) SCHOOL.

To the Parents (or Guardian)
of..........*Esther Weigh*

DEAR SIR (OR MADAM),

  I have to inform you that your child is qualified for admission to the above-named School.

  The Middle School has for its object the strengthening and improvement of the ordinary English Subjects (English, Geography, History), Mathematics and the elements of Science, and aims at teaching them to older children under more favourable conditions than exist in the ordinary Elementary School. There is also provision for instruction in Handicraft for the Boys and Domestic work for the Girls.

  If you desire your child to take advantage of this advanced instruction, will you kindly arrange for him (her) to attend at the School at 9-0 a.m. on Monday, the 8th April, 1929.

  In order that children promoted to such a School should obtain full advantage from the course offered, it is essential they should remain there until at least the end of the term in which they attain the age of 14.

    Yours faithfully,
     J. H. HALLAM.
      Education Officer.

L & Co. 217 500 1889

Wombwell Middle School prefects, *c.* 1929. Back row, left to right: M. Senior, E. Beevers, N. Brookfield, J. Connolly. Middle row: E. Turton, E. Wilkinson, M. Beevors, M. Lingard. Front row: M. Colley, K. Myers and E. Gawthorpe. (*Esther Johnson*)

Left: An informal photograph of James 'Jammy' Hall, Darfield Church School headmaster, *c.* 1933. (*Betty Adams*)

Right: Studio photograph of Mr Hoyle, headmaster of Darfield Church School, *c.* 1910. (*Betty Adams*)

Wombwell High School, *c.* 1965. The new school buildings can be seen in the centre of the photograph. (*David Biffen*)

The successful Low Valley School football team of 1949. Back row, left to right: Alan Markham, Alan Gibbs, Alan Dale, Bill Marsden, Stan Hayes, Sid Hill, Roy Gawthorpe, Roy Wilding, Ernest Wainwright. Front row: Tom Williams, Billy Askin, Alf Dunn, Lawrence Smedley, John Gill. Sitting on floor: Kevin McHale (who became a professional footballer) and Roy Griffiths (schoolboy international). The adults (local helpers) are Sam Turton (left) and Cliff Rowe. (*Bill Marsden*)

Low Valley Junior School football team in 1968, proud winners of the Clarke Shield. Back row, left to right: Jack Betts, Ian Leech, Paul Butterworth, Brett Haligan, John Shepherd, Mick Williams, -?-. Front row: John Rotherham, Tex Guy, Lloyd Marshall, ? Molyneaux and Philip Cox. (*Colin Leech*)

Headteacher Miss Florence Yarwood and a happy class of senior girls at Barnsley Road Junior Mixed School (Wombwell), *c.* 1932. Back row, left to right: Zena Watson, Olive Burrows, Emma Rasburn, -?-, Peggy Hall, Hazel Wilkinson, Jessie Turton. Middle row: Norma Gommersall, Barbara Turnbull, -?-, Margaret Rose, Betty Hinchliffe, -?-, -?-, -?-. Front row: Margaret Holling, Sarah Green, ? Osborne, Dorothy Cookson, ? Crowther, Marjorie Trout, -?-. (*Zena Hudson*)

A delightful studio photograph of Elsie Small, aged nine, 1909. Elsie was one of the seven children (she had three brothers and three sisters) of William and Elizabeth Small who kept the Ash Inn at Wombwell for many years. Elsie married Robert Weston, a motor mechanic with the T. Burrows omnibus company (see page 116). Elsie died in 1993. (*Zena Hudson*)

The crowning of the May Queen, Deidre Varney, John Street School, Wombwell, *c.* 1948. (*David & Elaine Biffen*)

A very interesting school classroom photograph of 'soldiers and indians' from the camera of R.J. Short. Joe Short always seemed to have an excellent rapport with his subjects. The location is Shroggs Head Junior School, Darfield and the year about 1954, since one of the boy indians, David Shone (third from left, with bow and arrow), was born in 1948. Perhaps more individuals will be identified in due course. (*Geoffrey Shone/R.J. Short*)

Did you attend Darfield Church School during the immediate post-war years? If so, here are some of your teachers. Back row, left to right: Horace Pears, Renee Banks, Mrs Price, Mrs Taylor. Seated: Betty Adams, Bill Price (headteacher) and Dinah Pears. (*Betty Adams*)

Darfield Church School staff, *c.* 1964. Back row, left to right: Mary Tunstall, -?-, -?-. Front row: Dinah Pears, Betty Adams, Norman Shacklock (headteacher), Renee Banks and Norma Sharpe. (*Betty Adams*)

Darfield Church School staff, *c.* 1974. Back row, left to right (standing): Norma Sharpe, Janet Welford, Miss Hargate, Mr Hargreaves, Mrs Fawcett, two student teachers. Front row: Muriel Parrish, Betty Adams, Peter Spencer (headteacher), Dinah Pears and Mary Tunstall. (*Betty Adams*)

A delightfully informal photograph of a small group of children from Darfield Upperwood Primary School consisting of, left to right, Samantha Hepplestone, Che Finnerty, Summer La Rivere and Ryan Skiffington. The adults are Mrs Sue McHale and Mrs Judith Kendall-Holmes. The modern (2003) Christian names make an interesting contrast with children of generations past. (*Barnsley Chronicle*)

Another very pleasant informal photograph, 2003. The children from Wombwell Park Street Primary are, left to right, Jack Herbert, Courtney Stuart, Callum Clark, Adam Clayton, Leanne Clayton, Luke Raynor, Harry Smith and Bernadette Carter. The teacher is Mrs Butterworth. (*Barnsley Chronicle*)

Senior staff of Wombwell High School, at a social evening in 1964. (*David Biffen*)

The Shone brothers of Darfield. Left to right: David (b. 1948, now a travel agent in Halifax, Nova Scotia, Canada), Peter (b. 1950, now a hospital worker and living at Silkstone Common, Barnsley) and Stephen (b. 1954, now at Carlton and employed at Beatson Clark's glass company). (*Geoffrey Shone*)

2

Pits All Around Us

Two ladies, believed to be from a cast of a local pantomime, visit Darfield Main in
about 1966. The escorts are miners John Reeves (left) and Neil Robinson.
(*Malcolm Robinson*)

Darfield Main was also known as Low Valley Colliery because of its location between Darfield and Wombwell. This early postcard (and the one below) provides us with a close view of the headgear, associated buildings and yard, stacked with timber. Two shafts were sunk to the Barnsley Bed in 1856. In 1872 a serious fire cast some doubt on the pit's future (see page 91 of the first volume of *Darfield & Wombwell*) but the owners overcame this and amalgamation with its arch rival, neighbouring Mitchell's Main, took place in about 1900. Although interrupted by the First World War, a new deeper shaft was sunk to extend the life of the pit, to the Thorncliffe Seam, also allowing access to a variety of other seams. The Meltonfield and Beamshaw Seams were important in the development from the 1930s. Further modernisation occurred after nationalisation, and new workings, in the Winter Seam, were opened, Darfield Main becoming noted for its high quality coking coal and record production figures in the 1950s. There was an extensive and expensive reconstruction scheme in the 1980s but by 1986 the pit was merged with Houghton and closed in 1989. (*Old Barnsley/Malcolm Hambleton*)

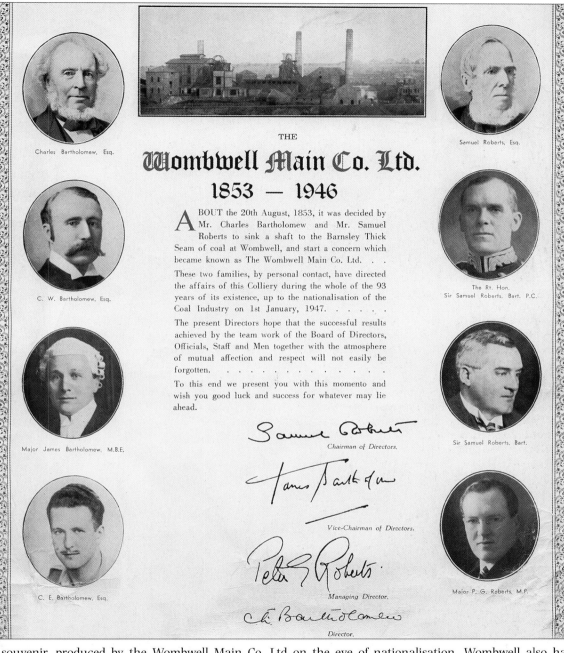

Charles Bartholomew, Esq.

Samuel Roberts, Esq.

THE

Wombwell Main Co. Ltd.
1853 — 1946

ABOUT the 20th August, 1853, it was decided by Mr. Charles Bartholomew and Mr. Samuel Roberts to sink a shaft to the Barnsley Thick Seam of coal at Wombwell, and start a concern which became known as The Wombwell Main Co. Ltd. . .

These two families, by personal contact, have directed the affairs of this Colliery during the whole of the 93 years of its existence, up to the nationalisation of the Coal Industry on 1st January, 1947. . . . . . .

The present Directors hope that the successful results achieved by the team work of the Board of Directors, Officials, Staff and Men together with the atmosphere of mutual affection and respect will not easily be forgotten. . . . .

To this end we present you with this momento and wish you good luck and success for whatever may lie ahead.

Chairman of Directors.

Vice-Chairman of Directors.

Managing Director.

Director.

C. W. Bartholomew, Esq.

The Rt. Hon.
Sir Samuel Roberts, Bart. P.C.

Major James Bartholomew, M.B.E.

Sir Samuel Roberts, Bart.

C. E. Bartholomew, Esq.

Major P. G. Roberts, M.P.

A souvenir, produced by the Wombwell Main Co. Ltd on the eve of nationalisation. Wombwell also had terrible problems with fires but, like Darfield, it developed a well-earned reputation for its coal, particularly for steam-power. By the end of the nineteenth century the complex included extensive coke ovens. Wombwell Main was one of the many Barnsley pits that shut during the Robens era, closing in 1969. *Brian Elliott)*

Members of the Darfield Main branch of the Yorkshire NUM parade their banner and sashes, probably in the 1920s. A superb photograph, important for our local social history, by Joe Short. (*R.J. Short/Anna@Drop Inn, Low Valley*)

A small group of young Houghton Main/Dearne Valley miners, several with blackened faces, pause for a local photographer by the Bridge Walk at Little Houghton, *c.* 1910. (*Old Barnsley*)

An interesting view of Cortonwood Colliery at the height of the 1984–5 miners' strike. The white vans in the far distance (right) are a convey of police heading for Brampton village. Looking over the miners' allotments there is a field which has medieval ridge and furrow. However, the entire landscape has now been transformed beyond recognition. (*Arthur Wakefield*)

Mitchell Main Colliery operated at the edge of Wombwell from the mid-1870s until 1956. (*Malcolm Hambleton*)

A rare photograph showing men at the entrance of one of the less well-known pits of the Barnsley area, Billingley Drift Mine. The small team of men have been identified as, left to right, Mr Morton (undermanager), Harry Hopkinson, Arthur Fereday (deputy), Joe Hays (fitter), Sid Cook (pit top worker), Harry Lockwood (ripper), Les Hall (ripper). Seated: Arthur Cutts (van driver). (*Lynn Bembridge*)

Miner's children, Rose and Emma Short playing on a delivery of coal in the backs of terraced properties, in 1924 at Millmoor Terrace, Low Valley. (*R.J. Short/NUM*)

n underground scene at Dearne Valley Colliery,
o. 2 Paddy Station, with a man-riding train in the
ation. The pump-man's lamp can be seen hanging
o the right, while he is visiting no. 2 Evans pump.
his photograph is by Joe Walker of Highgate,
oldthorpe. (*Colin Massingham*)

ne no. 2 tower winder at Houghton Main,
otographed by Colin Massingham in 1982. British
oal closed this old pit in late 1993 with the loss of
·0 jobs and, despite protests, its architecturally
teresting and historically important surface
ildings were demolished and the site cleared.
olin Massingham)

Police and pickets clash during the miners' strike at Middlecliffe on 1 February 1985. Pickets can be seen on the road and in the car park of Middlecliffe Working Men's Club (above, right) and the police can be seen wearing helmets and using riot shields by Scott's corner shop (below). (*Arthur Wakefield*)

Terence Picken, a regular member of the famous 'Alamo' picket outside Cortonwood Colliery, displays a commemorative plate relating to his pit and the year-long strike. (*Brian Elliott*)

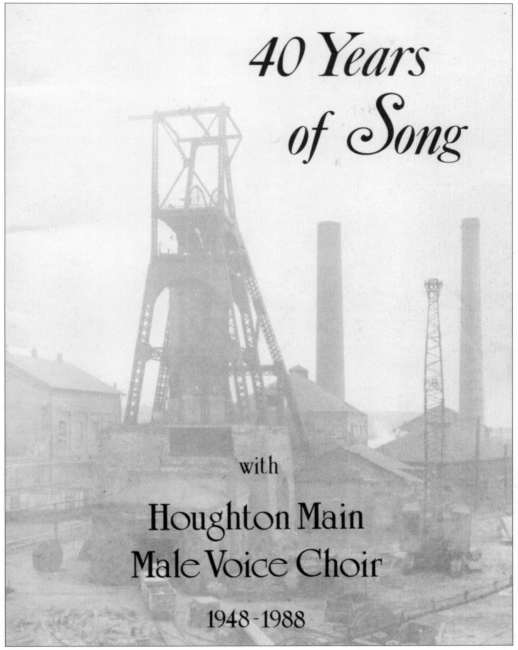

40 Years of Song

with

Houghton Main Male Voice Choir

1948-1988

The front cover of a commemorative brochure celebrating the fortieth anniversary of Houghton Male Voice Choir, 1988. Members then included Arthur Goldthorpe, Ernest Horbury, William Booth, Derrick Spink (musical director), Elizabeth Spink (accompanist), Edmund Turner, Percy Hargate, Ernest Smith, Robert Dixon, Tom Jeff, Jim Richardson, Clarrie Jones, Stan Harrison, Ken Hanks, Fred Immison, Jim Cousins, John Wotherspoon, Arthur Wakefield, Des Haynes, William Gleadhall, John Foss, Alvin Thorpe, Jim Gallacher, John Allott, John Sawyer, George Marlow, Steve Watson, Stuart Hampshire, Mick Finean, Fred Gillott, Roy Micklethwaite, Len Ibbeson, Arthur Singleton, George Wilson and Ronald Wakefield. (*Arthur Wakefield*)

Darfield Main's successful first aid team, winners of the prestigious Lane Fox Shield, *c.* 1958. Back row, left to right: -?-, Chris Thorpe. Front row: Malcolm Robinson, Ted Drury (coach), Mick Withers and Peter Alderson. (*Malcolm Robinson*)

Darfield Main NUM officials and Coal Board VIPs, *c.* 1974. Back row, left to right: Bob Cartledge, ? Pearson ? Machin (regional manager). Front row: John Reeves, Neil Robinson (pit deputy), Derek Ezra (NC chairman) and Derek Reeves. (*Malcolm Robinson*)

3

Church & Chapel

Looking very smart, male members of the Bible Class assemble for their photograph to be taken outside Darfield churchyard, *c.* 1912. Most of the men are wearing fashionable straw boaters but the younger ones prefer flat caps. Some of the more senior and authoritative men wear the customary bowler hat, often a sign of supervision or status. Stiff white collars and waistcoats complete the Sunday-best look. (*Betty Adams*)

Representing your church or chapel as a football or cricket player was a popular activity for many young men. Here are the Wombwell Wesleyan Chapel football team pictured during the 1915/16 season. Sixteen-year-old Stuart Parker is seated on the extreme right. Most of these young lads were probably miners but one wonders if any saw service in the First World War. The chapel on High Street was demolished, replaced by Burton Buildings. (*Mrs G. Wood*)

Darfield Bible Class football team, 1930s. They played a series of home and away fixtures, each followed with a social evening. For many people, social life revolved around the church and chapel. Those identified include Maurice Upton, Reg Dove, Gilbert Welford (in suit and cap), Dick Turpin, Albert Stansfield, George Vamplew and Tommy Hilton. (*Betty Adams*)

Team and officials of Houghton Wesleyan Foootball Club during the 1931/2 season. The goalkeeper is John Selbourne and to his left is 'Wigley' John Willie Leech (b. 1891) standing wearing overcoat and scarf on the far right. Others identified include Reg Taylor, standing tenth from left, the well-known chapel choirmaster whose wife was the organist. The photograph is believed to have been taken at the 'Duckie' field where football, cricket and nips were played. Their happy faces suggest that photographer Joe Short was sharing a joke with the team. (*R.J. Short/Colin Leech*)

A commemorative brochure for the Service of Thanksgiving for the opening and dedication of the new Darfield Church Hall (former Empire Cinema) in 1957. When the service was completed the choir and procession left the church for the hall chanting the *Te Deum*. (*Esther Johnson*)

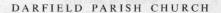

DARFIELD PARISH CHURCH

Service of Thanksgiving

On the occasion of the

OPENING AND DEDICATION

of

THE NEW CHURCH HALL

on

Saturday, November 9th., 1957

PREACHER:
The Right Rev. G. V. GERARD C.B.E., M.C., M.A.
(Assistant Bishop of Sheffield)

OPENER:
Major A. R. Keeping

WILFRED HOWARD, RECTOR
CHURCHWARDENS
VINCENT H. GOODALL   S. NORMAN SHAW

THIS FORM OF SERVICE MAY BE TAKEN AWAY

ALL SAINTS PARISH CHURCH, DARFIELD

A THANKSGIVING

FOR THE RESTORATION OF THE CHURCH

22nd - 28th September 1977

A later thanksgiving service, on this occasion for the completion of the restoration of All Saints' parish church, Darfield, in 1977. The Rector was the Revd John Batty and his assistant curate was the Revd C. Horseman. (*Betty Adams*)

Local people gather together for a very special occasion, a thanksgiving service towards the end of the First World War, at Low Valley Primitive Methodist Church (now Valley Methodist), on 24 June 1918. Note the fashionable wide-brimmed hats worn by most of the women, and the white stiff-collars endured by most of the gentlemen. It would be pleasing to receive more information relating to this splendid photograph. (*J.Parkin/W.Marsden*)

A presentation of a gift of candlesticks from Darfield Bible Class to Canon Sorby on his seventieth birthday in 1930. On the stage, left to right: George Herbert Galloway, Canon Sorby, Walter Briggs, Gilbert Welford and Alfred Rooke. Seated: -?-, Miss Dransfield, Joan Camplejohn, Sonia Powell, Kate Dove, Flora Davies (Conservative, JP), Mrs Briggs, Betty Welford (in Mexborough Grammar School uniform) and Geraldine Pearce.
(*Betty Adams*)

Canon Alfred Ernest Sorby, the much respected and well-loved rector of Darfield, appointed in 1892. Margaret Mann (née Longden) remembered him as a 'tall, upright man, a model of Christianity and a shining example of the Anglican ministry'; and also paid tribute to his 'limitless devotion and courage', particularly in regard to his stand in the famous Ascension Day Case when he successfully campaigned for the rights of parents of Darfield and the whole country for this special day in the church calendar. (*Margaret Mann*)

arfield Bible Class
icket team and
pporters outside
iddlewood Hall,
1910. The women
the back row are
earing huge hats.
he brims and size of
dies hats had just
out reached their
aximum at this
ne. More
formation about
e identities of
dividuals would be
preciated. The flat-
pped umpire on
e extreme right is
r Welford.
etty Adams)

very happy group of George Street Methodists (Low Valley) ladies are captured by the ever-present camera
Joe Short in this garden party, believed to be at Mill House, in 1951. (*R.J. Short/Bill Marsden*)

This Edwardian postcard is of the then newly built Barnsley Road Primitive Methodist Church at Wombwell. The tall tower continues to be a distinctive landmark. (*Brian Elliott*)

Newly weds David and Elaine Biffen (née Newsome) and guests, at Barnsley Road Methodist Church, in 1969. Left to right: Terry Simpson, Frank Farnhill, Irene Newsome, Dave Bullet, Brian Elliott (author), David Biffen and Elaine Biffen. (*David Biffen/Sherwood Studios*)

The Revd N. Morton and members of George Street Methodist Church Youth Club, mid-1950s. Back row, left to right: Sam Vamplew, Gordon Yates, Donald Brookes, James Theaker, Alan Lawson. Middle row: Gwen Simms, Wendy Elliott, Pat Wilkinson, Mary Huddart, Beryl Fisher, Geoff Bell, William Marsden. Front row: James Rowe (only half shown), Gladys Smallman, -?-, ? Beresford, the Revd N. Morton, Glynnis Walker and Janet Cousins. Another excellent photograph from R.J. Short of Wombwell. (*R.J. Short/Bill Marsden*)

George Street Methodists make a presentation to the Revd Norris Foster, August 1948. Back row, left right: Mrs Alters, Kath Shaw, Mrs Carver, Mrs Powell, Mrs Smallman, Mrs Freeman, Jim Rowe. Middle row Agnes Lee, ? Lee, Dorothy Smallman, Gladys Taylor, Jean Bamford, Glynnis Walker. Front row: unknown Oxley Powell is making the presentation of a table lamp. (*Bill Marsden*)

George Street Youth Clu Hike, Easter Monday, 1956, at Hope station, Derbyshire. Back row, le to right: ? Jackson, Sadi Westgarth, Ken Theake John Yates, Maureen ?, Pam Thompson, Nancy Gordon Yates, Glynnis Walker, Sam Vamplew, James Theaker, Alan Lawson. Front row: Joa Cousins, Alan Greenho -?-, Michael Norton, Janet Cousins, Beryl Fisher, Mary Huddart, Connie ?, William Marsden, Donald Brookes, Christine Bisby and Harry Butchers. (*Bill Marsden*)

chapels from George
Street (Low Valley),
Great Houghton
and Wisewood
(Sheffield) at a sixth
birthday event,
11 September 1953.
(*R.J. Short/Bill
Marsden*)

Low Valley Methodists (Snape Hill and George Street) enjoy preparations for the annual Whit Sing in the 1950s. Geoffrey Shone is at the 'mobile' organ. (*Geoff Shone*)

Mr A.C. Vaughan (centre, holding clock) receives a 'fifty years' service award from the National Sunday School president, Mr M. Guest, at Snape Hill (Valley Methodist Church in 1961. Mrs Vaughan is on the extreme left of the group and organist Geoffrey Shone (centre, right, also holding certificate assists with the happy ceremony. (*George Shone*)

This photograph, taken at Barnsley Road Methodist Church, in 1966, shows Tom Gibson preparing a slide presentation for fellow teenage members. (*David Biffen*)

Several members of the cast of the passion play, *Simon Peter*, held at the New Darfield Church Hall, Easter, 1961. Left to right: Jack Booth, Martyn Johnson, Geoff Shaw, Carol Dove, Gillian Barnley and Christine Gleadon.
(*Esther Johnson*/Sheffield Telegraph & Star)

The Revd and Mrs Julian Blakeley of Darfield, at the 1999 Christmas Fair, Valley Methodist Church.
(*Bill Marsden*)

Valley Methodist Church's most senior member was Ethel Craven who died a few years ago, aged 102. (*Bill Marsden*)

The Valley Chapel 'washing up/kitchen team'. Left to right: Gwen Beresford, Gladys Smallman and Bill Waddington. (*Bill Marsden*)

The popular monthly 'Men's Breakfast' at Valley Methodist Church, Saturday 4 January 2003. Left to right: Sam Vamplew, Bill Hinds, Donald Wiley, Colin Leech, Jim Bottom, Derek Empsall and Geoff Shone. (*Bill Marsden*)

The Methodist Women's Club enjoys a tea party at the George Hotel (corner pub), *c.* 1950. At or near the back, left to right: -?-, Mrs Hardcastle, Mabeth Timberlake (with teapot), Muriel Pickersgill, Dorothy Crookes, -?-, Mona Crookes (with teapot), Annie Sykes, -?-. Front: Mrs Crookes (landlady, drinking tea), -?- and Ella Marsden. (*R.J. Short/Bill Marsden*)

Another superb photograph from the camera of Joe Short. Low Valley Methodist women are shown preparing sandwiches for a chapel event in the 1950s. Note the 'pinnies' and the floral dresses. (*R.J. Short/Bill Marsden*)

Mount Tabor Methodist Church Sunday School, possibly at a Whit Sing, *c.* 1953. Those identified include Alan Beck, Lol Smith, Ronnie Trout, Barry Durham, Ian Cooling, Trevor Burgin, Barry Picker, Alan Fowler, Alan Venables, Malcolm Robinson, Neil Robinson, Gordon Kitchen, John Kitchen, Kathleen Tutill, Jean Evison, Granville Myers, Michael Crowcroft, Peter Berry, John Norton, Edna Gardner, Brian Bristow, Robert Tate and Dennis Rolf. Among the adults and Sunday school teachers are Irving Fairhurst, Harold Guest and Mr Copeland. (*Alan Beck*)

The Mount Tabor Methodist Church, 2003, which continues to function, though with a much smaller congregation than in the 1950s. (*Brian Elliott*)

4

Darfield &
Wombwell Memories

This Hambleton family photograph was taken outside 17 Church Street, Darfield, during the First World War. Mrs Annie Grange (previously Hambleton) is the senior lady at the centre of the group. She had married Reuben Hambleton (1866–1902), who, like many Darfield incomers, originated from Staffordshire, at Darfield parish church on 28 May 1888. After Reuben's death she married Ernest Grange at Barnsley Register Office, on Christmas Eve, 1908. Reuben and Annie's adult children shown on the photograph are, back row, left to right, William (1902–87), Jim (1896–1970, in army uniform), Reuben (1899–1970) and Lily (1898–1918). Front row: to Annie's right Margaret (1894–?) and on her left side, Nellie (1888–?). Annie's maiden name was Smith and she originated from Heath Common, near Wakefield. Another one of her sons, George, was serving in the army in India at the time this photograph was taken. (*Malcolm Hambleton*)

Hedley Longden, aged ten, in 1906, resplendent in his Penistone Grammar School uniform. (*Jim Longden*)

Memories of Hedley Longden (1896–1986) by his daughter, Margaret Mann.

My father, Hedley Longden, was the youngest in a family of ten, living in a mid-terrace house in School Street, Darfield. His father and two of his brothers were miners and his five sisters were 'in service'. His mother could neither read nor write. Working-class people in those days had little prospect of academic education but, against all the odds, my father obtained a place at Penistone Grammar School. The family had somehow clubbed together to pay the fees for him to be a boarder at the school. There were no buses and the daily train fare would have been too expensive.

On leaving Penistone Grammar, in 1911, Father started work as an office boy at Houghton Main Colliery, cycling every morning from the pit to Banks Hall, Cawthorne, delivering the post to John Brass, the colliery owner. He worked his way up to become chief sales accountant at the colliery.

At the outbreak of the First World War Father joined the Royal Engineers, serving in Baghdad, Mesopotamia (modern-day Iraq). In 1920 he married Elizabeth Cherry of Quarry Hills, Darfield, where he bought a cottage from the Middlewood estate, and they lived there for the rest of their lives. They had two children – James and me.

The sacrifices made by his family that enabled him to have a grammar school education made a lasting impression on my father. I think he felt an obligation to serve fellow men who had not had a similar opportunity. He was well remembered as secretary to the Darfield Nursing Association (1924–48) and from the 1920s until 1970 he was clerk to the trustees of the Darfield branch of the Alice Adams Charity, taking money to needy widows. He also served in the Darfield ARP throughout the Second World War.

Left: Hedley Longden in the uniform of the Royal Engineers, *c.* 1914. (*Margaret Mann*)

Right: This photograph of Hedley Longden was taken while he was serving in Basra, Iraq, in 1915 and signed 'love from Hed' on the back. In later life Hedley often told his children that the Basra/Baghdad area would be a place where a future world war would start. (*Jim Longden*)

School Street, Darfield, from a postcard posted in Darfield in 1924. The house where Hedley Longden lived as a boy may have been the one where the figure of a man, standing in a front garden and wearing a white shirt, is just visible. (*Margaret Mann*)

Left: Mary and James Longden (parents of Hedley) at their son's wedding, 11 September 1920. (*Margaret Mann*)

Right: Newly weds Elizabeth (née Cherry) and Hedley Longden, on a long walk over Houghton Common. Hedley looks smart in his white collar and dark tie. The trilby and cane typify the early 1920s as does Elizabeth's fox fur. (*Margaret Mann*)

Houghton Main Colliery office staff, *c.* 1925, not long before the miners' strike. Back row, left to right Hedley Longden, Tommy Roberts (office boy), Frank Batty, Rowland Pearson and Frank Windle. Front row John Brass Jnr and John Brass Snr, colliery owner. (*Jim Longden*)

Committee and friends at the opening ceremony of the Darfield Nurses' Home, 21 May 1914. Situated in Barnsley Road, the Nurses' Home was the gift of Charles Howard Taylor of Middlewood Hall, who was presented with a gold key by Mrs J. Mitchell on behalf of the committee. The building was conveyed to a new body of trustees in 1916, including Hedley Longden who was to become its long-serving secretary. Individual subscriptions (collected by volunteers such as Hedley) stood originally at 1*d* a week, increasing to 2*d* in 1920. Understandably, income dropped significantly during the miners' strike of 1926. (*Margaret Mann*)

The final committee of the Darfield Nursing Association. Under the National Health Service Act of 1948 the authority of the trustees passed to the West Riding County Council, after almost thirty-five years of home nursing for the sick of Darfield and district. (*Margaret Mann*)

**From flour boy to chief education welfare officer: a tribute to Alec Clarney (1911–2001)
by Margaret Mann.**

The lives of many older and former residents of Darfield have been touched by the work and influence of Alec Clarney who died in Bude, Cornwall, aged eighty-nine, in 2001. Born in Owram Street, he was a son of County Alderman Harry Clarney and a pupil at Low Valley Council School, gaining a scholarship to Wath Grammar School. His first job was as a flour boy at the Barnsley British Co-operative Society branch in Edward Street, Darfield.

When war broke out in 1939 Alec joined the RAF, serving in the SIB (Special Investigation Branch) in Normandy, Belgium, Holland and Germany. Afterwards he joined the West Riding County Council as a local education welfare officer. His proven abilities resulted in promotion to chief education welfare officer. When local government was reorganised in 1974 he became superintendent education welfare officer for Wakefield MDC. His numerous professional achievements include the Presidency of the Education Welfare Officers' Association and he represented Yorkshire on the national committee of NALGO (National Association of Local Government Officers).

Alec Clarney was a lifelong member of the Labour Party and was elected the first secretary of the Darfield branch, and later its chairman. He was a councillor for the old Darfield Urban District Council and represented the community on many committees and village organisations. His work in improving facilities for older people has been much appreciated. One of his ambitions which he saw to fruition was the building of the Old People's Centre in Illsley Road, in about 1970.

The Darfield Amenity Society benefited from his experience; indeed he was a founder member and served as chairman and vice-chairman. He was also a founder member of the Police Liaison Committee, and served as secretary to the Friends of Havenfield.

As a young man Alec was a player and stage manager of the Darfield Dramatic Society and was a member of the Darfield Walking Club. Alec Clarney had a great interest in local history, accumulated a great deal of knowledge and compiled notes about the village and parish of Darfield.

A studio photograph showing Alec Clarney (far left) with his brothers Harry (centre) and Jack as young children in 1913. (*Margaret Mann*)

A sensitive portrait of Alec Clarney, from the studio of young Wombwell photographer Joe Short, *c.* 1938, just before war service. (*Margaret Mann*)

Sergeant Alec Clarney in RAF uniform (85 Group, 2nd Tactical Airforce) in Brussels, 1945. (*Margaret Mann*)

Alec became chairman of Darfield UDC not long after this portrait from about 1950 was taken. (*Margaret Mann*)

Alec in the early 1970s when he was chief education welfare officer for West Riding County Council. (*Margaret Mann*)

Mining Memories of Geoffrey Shone

Geoffrey, now aged seventy-seven, worked at Houghton Main Colliery for forty-two years (1931–83) He has been organist at Valley Chapel since about 1954 and sang in the Houghton Main Male Voice Choir and now the Wombwell Mixed Choir.

I was born at 6 Havelock Street (off Snape Hill) in Low Valley on 5 September 1926. I was always known as a 'strike baby'. My parents were Beatrice Ellen (b. 1896) and Enoch (b. 1866) Mother was born in Great Houghton but Dad came from Tipton in Staffordshire. Father had a Black Country accent and never lost it. He settled at Wath for a while and then moved to Low Valley, finding work at Houghton Main where he worked as a filler and much later as an engine driver. He continued working underground until the age of seventy-nine, occasionally working a double shift even in his seventies.

I went to Darfield Council School, at the bottom of Snape Hill, across from the Methodist chapel. I left school, aged fourteen, on the Friday and started work at Houghton Main pit on the Monday. Sammy Bellamy, who was the undermanager, ran a class on safety measures which I attended and he got me a job. On my first morning I reported to the pit and went down straight away. I was very apprehensive and felt lost, even though my dad and step brothers worked there From the pit bottom I went to the Box Hole (underground office) and I was told to go to Mr Baxter who was in charge of the timber. 'Old Doc Baxter' as he was known, lived in Hough Lane, Wombwell. He had a little goatee beard and said to me, 'Right, lad, go down to the face and see what the men want'. I did not really understand what a face was. I had to write in chalk on a piece of wood how many props, etc. the men needed, taking the props to them. It was hard work, then a case of getting home, bathed, and I dropped off to sleep when having my dinner For a time I worked with my oldest brother Enoch, and his son, Arnold, and a team of repair men. At snap time we would sometimes sit down and start singing. One of my favourites was 'Guide Me Oh Thou Great Redeemer'. One Christmas we sat down and sang carols.

I wore ordinary home clothes, old trousers, boots, a shirt and a flat cap. We had to buy our own tools. They provided us with an electric lamp, about six inches high, like a lighthouse, or an oil lamp and you were really in the dark if it went out. You could not see your hand in front of you. For my snap I took a bottle of water and sandwiches, jam or dripping, or maybe sliced apple or marmalade.

I worked in the Parkgate Seam for about a year and then moved to the Melton Field, working in the pit bottom and then on the haulage, packing and putting empties (tubs) on to the roadway From then on I went to the face as a tension lad, keeping the belts running free. I did this for several years and then went back on to the haulage, lashing tubs on to the main road, empties going down or full ones coming up. For several years I was a pony driver. Some were good to drive but others were terrible. Mack was my favourite, and then there was Victor, Pablo and Snowy (a real devil who would take the weight but refuse to pull). Later I worked as a wireman, helping the electricians, working there until I damaged my back. I was pulling a cable tight when my foot slipped and was off work twelve months. I still suffer with it now. When I was on the haulage I also got my little finger trapped and was five months off work, the finger having to be removed I got six pence per week compensation but was told I had been overpaid, so had to pay it all back.

Before the war Houghton Main was a private pit, belonging to the Taylor family. I remember Vesting Day (nationalisation, 1 January 1947) when I was on the afternoon shift. I went down a private pit and came up an NCB worker but it made little difference.

The first manager I remember was Mr Taylor, then there was Mr Mackie who was the Parkgate undermanager (and later manager) and Mr Bellamy, undermanager in Melton Field. One of the Beamshaw undermanagers was George Thompson who lived in Havelock Street. Mr Fox was an undermanager in the Meltonfield and became manager.

A terrible explosion took place in the Newhill Seam on 12 June 1975 when two of my mates, electricians Ray Copperwheat and Len Baker, were killed (along with three others: Richard Bannister, a pumpman, and deputies Irvin Lakin and Arnold Williamson). Several others were badly injured. I had come home from my day-shift on the surface and Ray and Len were on the six o'clock (night) shift. The next morning we were all stunned. There were emergency vehicles here and the rescue team in the pit yard. One of the deceased was recognised by a Bible he always carried. Visitors included the [Secretary of State for Energy] MP Tony Benn, the union compensation secretary Arthur Scargill, NUM President Joe Gormley and NCB Chairman Derek Ezra. There were television and newspaper reporters. The pit closed for a short while but we had to carry on working as soon as possible. We wanted to attend Ray and Len's funeral but were not allowed, being told that time off would have meant a breach of contract.

After my back accident in 1963 I got a lighter job on the surface, working in the electrical shop, until retiring in 1983, a few months before the miners' strike. On my last day at work I emptied my locker and clocked off and that was it. No ceremony or presentation but I was relieved that my retirement had arrived at last.

Beatrice Ellen and Enoch Shone with children Muriel and Geoffrey, 1940s. Geoffrey recalled that his father was one of the miners who would never bath at the pit (pithead baths were built at Houghton in 1931) but preferred a 'good swill' in the kitchen sink coupled with a weekly 'tin bath'. In 1947 the Shones 'flitted' to Woodall Road, to a three-bedroomed house with a bathroom. Geoff described this as 'like moving to a palace'. (Geoffrey Shone)

Geoffrey Shone and his younger sister, Muriel, outside the front door of their terraced house, 6 Havelock Street, early 1930s. (*Geoffrey Shone*)

The Shone family calls at a photographer's studio on a day trip to Blackpool, *c.* 1938. Note the bandage on young Geoffrey's leg. He was still recovering, after five months in hospital, from a nasty accident following a blackberrying expedition to Darfield Quarry, when he slipped and broke a leg. (*Geoffrey Shone*)

Geoffrey Shone at the Valley Chapel organ, 1960s. (*Geoffrey Shone*)

Houghton Main colliery as it appeared in the early 1900s. Two shafts were sunk between 1871 and 1873, and the famous Barnsley Seam reached at 525 yards. The pit was well situated, being adjacent to the LMS railway and easily served by sidings. In 1909, about the time this photograph was taken, a staple shaft was sunk from the Melton Field Seam to the Barnsley Seam and various improvements continued during the 1920s. By the 1930s output from the working of four seams was up to 4,000 tons per day, from hand-got and mechanised faces. It was a big pit, employing around 2,000 men, many of the older ones originating from the West Midlands. (*Old Barnsley*)

Hilda Perrin Remembers

Hilda Perrin is the oldest resident in the Barnsley area, having celebrated her 107th birthday in Jun 2003. This extract is based on an interview recorded on 20 March 2003, and also from Hilda's writte memoirs. Family history details are from the research of Barbara Sanders, née Camplejohn.

My name is Edith Perrin (née Camplejohn) and I was born on 20 June 1896 when Queen Victori was on the throne. She was a lovely queen. After she died in 1901 I can remember all th celebrations in honour of the new king, Edward VII. I ran across the road to the sports field nea where we lived in Low Valley, at the bottom of Snape Hill. My mother struggled to put a big fla out of our bedroom window. My father, Anthony Camplejohn (1865–1938), was born i Alderney in the Channel Islands and Mother's name was Maria Ward (1867–1936). I had eigh brothers. They were Colin (b. 1889), Walter (b. 1890), Amos (b. 1892), Sidney (b. 1894), Irvin (b. 1900), Anthony (b. 1904) and Eric. The there was me (b. 1896) and my younger siste Nora (b. 1907). My parents came over to Lo Valley because of the pits.

I went to Low Valley Mission School (a da school for infants and girls of St Matthew Mission Church). Canon Sorby (the Revd Albe Ernest Sorby MA) was always very nice. He use to visit my mother and give us advice. When h came to visit the school I went home a lunchtime and polished my shoes and put on clean white apron. We all wore those. I stood o the back row and he picked me out as th 'cleanest girl' in the class and gave me sixpenc I did value that sixpence.

I had an uncle and aunt who kept a farm they were the Swifts. I used to go there in morning with a jug and fetch some fresh mil My sister Nora went out selling milk.

When I was a girl we lived in a two bedroomed rented property. I always had to wor at home, even after I got married. My moth used to say she kept us all on a pound a wee housekeeping, but I just don't know how sh managed. We never bought a loaf of brea everything was baked and mother made som wonderful fruit pies. I used to have to scrub th floors as there were no carpets, just rugs. I g up early as I had to get the boys out of bed, clea the house and polish shoes and on Sunda

A *carte-de-visite* photograph of Hilda Camplejohn, aged about six, 1902. (*Hilda Perrin*)

ange five beds. I didn't have time for a
unday dinner, just a bit of Yorkshire pudding
efore going to the Bible Class at two in the
ternoon, at Darfield.

The Camplejohn brothers bought one of the
rst charabanc buses. It had solid tyres and a
mall three-step ladder to get in. The seats
ent right across the vehicle and they had to
ollect money from a narrow ledge (or
unning board') along the side of the
harabanc, even when it was still moving.

I can remember the first aeroplanes on show
Wombwell, looking to me like large kites.

I was eighteen years old when the First
World War started in 1914. Two of my
others joined up as drivers. Sidney drove
mbulances in France and Amos went to
alonika. They were very fortunate to get
ome in 1918. I met my intended husband,
illiam Henry Perrin, at the Church Bible
ass Christmas party. It was not love at first
ght but it grew. Our courtship was
terrupted when he joined the Barnsley Pals
attalion and was badly wounded and
ospitalised near Warrington. I was able to
sit him with his mother. Later I spent a week
ing nearby, staying at an old lady's cottage
d managed a few short walks with him in
e hospital grounds. When I had to leave his
ends in the ward sang, 'You've left behind a

Hilda Perrin celebrating her 100th birthday in
1997. She has a daughter, Peggy, three grand-
daughters and seven great-grandchildren. Hilda is
one of the few people who can remember the death
of Queen Victoria, and four monarchs have been
crowned in her lifetime. (*Peggy Shaw*)

oken doll'! Eventually he was discharged and came home but his right arm was not good, so he
uld not do heavy work.

We were married in Darfield church on 15 April 1920 at eight o'clock in the morning! Then
e had a breakfast/lunch at my mother's house, caught a bus to Wombwell and trains to
ignton for our honeymoon. We were there two weeks and it cost us £20. We came back to a
nall, rented house in New Street, paying 4s 6d a week. My husband's wages were £3 but we
anaged. He was a clerical worker at Houghton Main pit.

There were many sad events earlier in the century, especially in 1912 when the *Titanic* sunk
d the miners were on strike. Then we had more miners' strikes and another war against
ermany when Winston Churchill was Prime Minister. There was King Edward's abdication
d Princess Diana's tragic death. I am hoping for more peaceful years in the new century. I
ight have had it rough sometimes but I've had a happy life, so that's probably why I've lived
long.

Four Camplejohns, including John William ('Billie'), stand by their Karriercar grey charabanc, *c.* 1913. Hilda and her sister Nora Camplejohn may be the young ladies sitting on the front seat of vehicle C 7020. Joan Naylor (née Camplejohn) remembers that her father, John William (1890–1963), used to take his pigeons with him when he went on a chara excursion, so that if the vehicle broke down they would be released and his father, William Dowson, landlord of the Bricklayers Arms, would notice their return to the loft. Spare parts could then be sent to Billie. It was an efficient and fast method of communication long before the mobile phone! (*Joan Naylor/Barbara Sanders*)

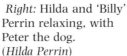

Left: A sensitive portrait of Miss Hilda Camplejohn, from the Barnsley studio of Denton and Co., *c.* 1916. (*Hilda Perrin*)

Right: Hilda and 'Billy' Perrin relaxing, with Peter the dog. (*Hilda Perrin*)

A delightful photograph of Hilda Amplejohn (front right) and three of her friends: Agnes Doby (back left), Hilda Harem (back right), and Eleanor Coe (front left), probably dating from the First World War. (*Hilda Perrin*)

William and Hilda Perrin and their daughter Peggy enjoy a day at the seaside at Bridlington, *c.* 1932. (*Hilda Perrin*)

Hilda Perrin, aged 106, photographed on 20 March 2003. (*Brian Elliott*)

Printing and Mining – Malcolm Hambleton

I was born at 6 John Street on 27 August 1932. My earliest memory is attending the infant and junior schools at the bottom of Snape Hill. Miss Snowden was the headmistress at the infants and the junior school headteacher was Mr Clayton.

My father, William Hambleton, was born in Grimethorpe in 1902, the same year as my mother, whose maiden name was Elizabeth Rodgers. She came from Silkstone.

Father may have been a miner as a young man but I always remember him working as a Co-op milkman. His round was mainly in and around Darfield but he did some deliveries to Wombwell, as I recall that on one occasion he had a bad fall, possibly in Gower Street, and gashed his eye, requiring several stitches. He used the old push carts, with two shafts and had to pull it manually. As well as bottles of milk, he delivered eggs and butter. Dad knew plenty of people in Darfield, though he identified many of his customers by their Co-op check numbers!

Our house was two-up and two-down, for five of us. There was a kitchen and a living room and shared outside toilets across the back yard. No hot water, just an old copper, but we had a fire of course.

There were no such thing as holidays for working-class people. You were lucky to go on a day trip to the seaside. One day we were on a day trip to Cleethorpes on a 'Tosh' Greenhow bus when the engine overheated and the radiator cap blew off. We all ended up looking for it. I also used to travel on Camplejohn's buses. It used to cost 5*d* when we went to watch Barnsley but we would often ride there and walk back, to save money.

I left Darfield Foulstone School when I was still aged thirteen in July, a month before my birthday. Straight away I went to the Labour Exchange and a chap just picked me and another young lad out and asked us if we fancied a job as a printer. I went to Taylor's printers at Station Road, Wombwell. Arthur Taylor, one of the bosses (there were four Taylor brothers who ran the business), interviewed me but I couldn't start until I was aged fourteen.

I was amazed when I saw the machinery for the first time. The machine shop was full but some machines were still covered up from the war; men were still returning from the army. The first machines that I worked on were Heidelbergs. I soon moved on to operating and setting the machine up. There was a wide range of printing jobs, anything from theatre and pantomime bills to income tax forms. It was always a big rush on a Friday night to get the bills off as they went all over the country. It was mucky work for your hands and overalls. Tom Bedford was the foreman and I remember Claud Skelton who was always singing. We used to get our legs pulled as young lads. Starting time was 7.45 a.m. until noon, then I used to dash home for my dinner, having to be back for 1 p.m. I would guess there must have been about a hundred people working there. It was a big works. There were three floors: packing department and book binding department and the machine shop floor which I was on, and then there was the 'comp' room for typesetting. Lithography was on the machine floor.

I didn't finish my apprenticeship because the wages were so poor. All my mates were earning more by working down the pit, so I decided to join them. I got a job at Dearne

Malcolm Hambleton, aged six, looking extremely smart, in John Street, *c.* 1938. Webster's corner shop is on the right and the other shop in view (with a group of young men in front) is Hammerton's on Snape Hill, though it may be closed. The lady sweeping the pavement outside her house may be Mrs Debney. (*Malcolm Hambleton*)

Valley Colliery, a drift mine. Before I started, Alec Dunn, one of the safety officers, asked me if played football. I told him that I played for Taylor's Printers. In the first match that I played befor I started at the pit I hurt my wrist in a tackle and had to have hospital treatment, so on my fir day I had to walk round with the safety officer, my arm being in a bandage.

After my first day underground I wondered what I had done and regretted leaving printing. O my first real day down Dearne Valley I was stretcher-carrying, someone had got hurt and we ha to get them out. Luckily, I was never involved in an accident.

I went pony driving until I got married. I had to look after the pony, hooking it on to empt tubs and bringing full ones away from the coal face. I still remember some of the horses' name There was George, Boxer, Sailor and Duke. Some were OK to work with but others were ver difficult. I worked with George a lot, a dappled grey, though the horses tended to stop with th jobs they were doing rather than staying with one man all the time. George was really funny a he always wanted to have a roll on the ground before he went anywhere. One of my mates wa Jack Marsh from Havelock Street, Low Valley. Then there was Len Powell, a Darfield lad, Ro Brewster from Houghton and Alvin Ella. I was keen to progress and learn mechanical skills suc as 'fitting'.

Mrs Elizabeth Hambleton, with children Malcolm, Iris (left) and Rita (right), on the front step of 6 John Street, c. 1942. (*Malcolm Hambleton*)

No. 6 John Street, shortly before demolition, in the late 1960s. (*Malcolm Hambleton*)

William Hambleton, Barnsley British Co-op milkman for over thirty years, outside 6 John Street. He married Elizabeth Rodgers at Darfield Parish Church on 6 June 1925, Canon Sorby performing the ceremony. The couple celebrated their golden wedding anniversary at their home, St Barbara's Road, Darfield. (*Malcolm Hambleton*)

Malcolm Hambleton, in his pit clothes, at the backs of John Street, with Snape Hill in the background, 1951. Note the boots and trousers tucked in his socks. No uniforms in those days, despite nationalisation. (*Malcolm Hambleton*)

There was an interlude. In the early fifties three of us volunteered to join up: Sam Roebuck (Navy), Alvin Ella (Guards) and myself. I served in the RAF. It got me out of the pit, but only for a few months as I was hospitalised, but after recovering returned straight down the pit, working on haulage.

After getting married in 1954 (I met my late wife, Maureen, who came from Grimethorpe, at the Ritz cinema in Barnsley one Sunday night). I moved to Ferrymoor Colliery, qualifying as a cutter, working there until 1967, but did not like it.

A neat line of Wombwell UDC Highway vehicles, along with their driver and superintendent, parade in the council yard. Part of the substantial works of Taylor's Printers can be seen in the background, 1950s. (*Old Barnsley*)

Malcolm Hambleton (right), with his son, David, outside their Shepley home, near Huddersfield, 27 January 2003. After leaving the pit in 1967, Malcolm was employed by Barnsley Corporation Waterworks Department in the fresh air of Scout Dyke Reservoir, near Penistone, where he was able to use his mechanical and maintenance skills in a far healthier environment. (*Brian Elliott*)

Darfield Main in the 1950s – Malcolm Robinson

was born on 17 October 1938 at Mexborough Montague Hospital. My parents lived at 63 Myers Street, Wombwell, across from the canal and Mitchells Main pit. The house was in a terrace. It had a little kitchen, one front room and two bedrooms. I just don't know how we managed as there were seven of us. We slept three in a bed [laughs] and I remember that two slept one way and one slept in the other direction. There was a tin bath and when it was used it was a big occasion! There was a copper for heating the water, but later on we got a gas boiler. There was an old Yorkshire range. We used to chop the sticks for making the fire and place them at the side of the range and they would be as dry as cinder, perfect for starting the fire. Lighting was by gas, using mantles. I had to run to the shop to get new ones, Parkin's shop at the top of the street. On Fridays I was sent to the Co-op for rations. I fetched the flour for baking and everything. Mother's writing was bad. One day she wrote 'one ounce of black barges' – she really meant tobacco!

My father's name was Alfred and my mother is called Mary. Her maiden name is Rowe. I have four brothers: Neil, Kenneth, Ray and Alfred. Dad worked at Darfield Main. He was a face-worker but became the onsetter at the pit bottom, organising men and materials going up and down. His father, George, was also a miner and may have worked at the same pit.

I went to John Street Junior School and then to Wombwell Modern School, leaving when I was fifteen. Dad said, 'I have got you a job, lad', but I wished he had never done it! But it did me good, working down the pit. I did my training at Brierley and Hemsworth College.

It was 1954 when I started. When I went down the pit the first time it was quite an experience. I was surprised how everything was so lit up at the pit bottom but the roadways got

A barge pauses on the wide but shallow Dearne & Dove Canal, by the timber yard of Mitchell Main Colliery, 1905. The gable end of the last house in Myers Street is just visible on the far left. Back-to-back miners' properties can also be seen on the right, almost within the pit yard. Note the washing strung out between the middens (toilets) and the canal fence. Quite a sizeable industrial complex had developed in this area during the last quarter of the nineteenth century, attracted by the canalside location and good rail links. Oldham Glass Bottle Works, its tallest chimney dating from 1899, is a distinctive landmark. (*Old Barnsley*)

narrower and lower as you progressed further into the workings. It could be twenty minutes or more to walk to your workplace.

I worked underground attending to the haulage, carrying pit props and other things that the men at the faces needed. They treated the young lads great but we had our legs pulled a lot. It did you good. I progressed to be a trainee cutter and then became a cutter, working on the face. At the age of seventeen I was earning good money. We got paid by piece-work. We would sit down with the deputy and what we had done and the rate and any extras would be calculated. I worked in the Beamshaw Seam and then the Melton Field. Beamshaw was less than three foot high, so we had to do a lot of crawling but you got used to it. One of the big hazards was the dust from the coal cutters and you had to be professional all the time, be aware of the dangers. Safety was so important. We had to be flexible as well – boring a hole for firing and seeing the belting, pulling the belt over to put the coal on and to run it off.

Malcolm and his teenage friends enjoy a drink in a Blackpool pub, *c.* 1956. Left to right: Terry Wroe, -?-, Malcolm Robinson and Geoff Barker. Malcolm recalls that Terry in particular was an outstanding Wombwell sportsman. (*Malcolm Robinson*)

My mother used to put my snap up: bread and dripping, bread and jam on different days. One day I was eating my sandwiches and she had put dripping on one side and jam on the other! I took a bottle of water to drink.

There was a lot of camaraderie. Halfway to our work place we used to sit down and have a rest and we told stories and had a chat. On one occasion I remember a new singer called Elvis Presley being talked about. The old miners said he would not last but I disagreed with them.

There were pit baths but some miners came home instead. Some of them did not like their backs being washed or showered because of superstition. I remember when my dad used to come home after he had showered. We sometimes would find him worn out, fast asleep by the stairs.

I did not dislike the job and the people that I worked with were great, but I began to be concerned about my future health because of the dust, so I decided to leave. I got a temporary job at Butlins and eventually worked for an insurance company. I progressed to become a manager which involved moving to Cheshire for a while.

I now live in Hemingfield with my wife Beryl who I first met at the Pavilion Pictures in Wombwell. I used to play a lot of football and cricket, but nowadays I keep busy playing bridge. I have become a Grand Master, take part in competitions and do some teaching. I also enjoy playing golf. I'll soon be sixty-five but play off a six handicap.

...ace celebrations in Myers ...reet, 1945. Everyone is having ...good time. The event was ...arted by a gun fired by ...rgeant Howson. (*Malcolm ...binson*)

A small group of young women, wearing 'pinnies', sit in the backs of Myers Street, *c*. 1950. They are: -?-, Kathleen Alderson, Mary Robinson (Malcolm's mother) and Lily Beck. (*Malcolm Robinson*)

...is first aid competition took ...ce at Wombwell, possibly in ...e hall of the secondary school, ...958. Those involved in the ...m included Chris Thorpe, ...lcolm Robinson and Peter ...derson. Dr Tom Bell is judging. ...alcolm Robinson)

Florence's Wombwell

My name is Florence Mabel Copeland and I was born at 20 Blythe Street, Wombwell o
20 September 1910, so I am ninety-three years old. My father's name was Tom Rollin and n
mother's maiden name was Dunn. I had two brothers, Jack and Tommy, and two sisters, Jess
and Edna, so there were seven of us, living in a terraced house, two-up and two down. From th
front door you walked into the 'house' and then into the kitchen. There were cellars where v
kept coal, bread and vegetables – and also the tin bath. We boiled pans of water on bath night o
an open fire. Mother bathed each of us in the peggy tub many a time after wash day! Toilets we
outside, shared with another family, and just two upstairs bedrooms.

Father, who was born in Wombwell, was a miner at Houghton Main. He used to say that I
walked as much underground as he did to get to work. I've seen him when he came home so tire

Florence Rollin (standing at the garden-side of the gate) and her younger sister, Edna (b. 1920), at their Thompson Road home in Wombwell, *c.* 1928. (*Florence Copeland*)

that he lay on the kitchen floor an
mother had to take his clogs off.
was all pick and shovel down the p
in those days.

Mother came from Staffordshir
moving here when she was abou
fourteen. My maternal grandfathe
John Dunn, came to Wombwell
work in the pits. My grandmothe
Hannah Dunn, had sevente
children of her own and brought u
six others besides. She lived
Stoneyford Road but earlier in Geor
Square.

My earliest memory was going
Barnsley Road Infants School whe
I was three or four when Miss Pri
was the teacher and Miss Garbu
the head. Later, I went to John Stre
Junior.

I was four when the First Wor
War started. Towards the end whe
there was no food getting throug
(submarines were sinking ships) d
used to queue for a bit of margari
and sometimes when he got to t
front there was nothing left. M
mother told me that she saw
Zeppelin.

I remember running errands f
neighbours. Most would give you

r shopping, though Mrs Bedford used to
ve me 3d. It was marvellous! I went to
e Co-op, the Maypole Dairy and Gallons
rocers) on High Street, and the Globe
a Co. (Park Street).

We had gas lighting so I went
opping for mantles and oil for the
raffin lamps, but we had candles to go
 bed. We always kept spares as you
ver knew when it would blob. The
raffin lamp was used if anyone was
orly.

Wombwell Feast was very popular, the
ghlight of the year, as nobody had
ough money for holidays. We used to
ake fruit cake and have a spring clean.
ere was a big fair, Tuby's. The fields
ar the police station were used and
fore that the field near the canal.

I was a regular chapelgoer, especially
 Mount Tabor on Barnsley Road. At
hit we assembled in the field at the
ck of the Empire. The Salvation Army
d the Wombwell Town Band used to
ay. We walked from the field up John
reet and then on Blythe Street, up
metery Road, carrying big banners.

I remember the 1926 miners' strike. I
d been working at the shirt factory
ice the age of fourteen (Sugden's,
ocks Lane, Barnsley).

Florence Copeland at her Wombwell home, 17 February
2003. (*Brian Elliott*)

There were no buses so we had to walk and try and get lifts from passing wagons or lorries.
was very hard for families. Dad was off work six months. I was earning 30s a week at the age
sixteen and thought I was keeping the family! We flitted to Thompson Road just before the
ike and had to make special arrangements to pay the rent.

Fred, my husband, worked at Houghton Main as an onsetter but worked in the medical room
wards the end of his life. We were married by the Revd Mr Blakeney on 16 September 1933,
ombwell Feast Saturday. There were about ten weddings on that day.

I was eighteen when I had my first holiday, to Blackpool for a week. Mostly we went to
ecar Park, Wombwell Woods, and Hoober Stand at Wentworth was popular for picnics.
ccasionally went on charabanc trips. There were Tommy Lee, Camplejohns and Burrows.

We only fetched a doctor if we were desperate as you had to pay. Dad joined the Oddfellows,
ying about 2d a week so as to cover the doctor's fees. It was Dr Pickup who lived at the

Gables at the top of Cemetery Road. Chemists made up their own medicines. If you had a cold
was a drop of 'compo' and you had to go to work no matter how you felt.

I worked at the shirt factory for nine years until I was married and then used to take in sewir
to help make ends meet as the pits were often on short time during the thirties.

After the start of the Second World War the sirens went off on the Sunday and there w
panic. We got gas masks and I was sat up in bed when the sirens started. Everyone came out
the avenue, off Summer Lane. My sister got married the year that the Germans blitzed Sheffiel
On some nights you could hear Sheffield being bombed. I did not want to work in munition
though did have to work a few days at Sheffield Brightside, but stopped as I was suffering fro
arthritis.

After the war I worked at Raven's in Barnsley, making blouses, etc., and then worked at Syke
garage on Barnsley Road with my sister operating the petrol pumps. I enjoyed working there un
I was seventy.

A superb view of Wombwell High Street, dating from the early years of the twentieth century. The Globe 1
Co.'s shop that Florence Copeland remembers is clearly visible at the Church Street junction, on the l
Guest's pawnbroking emporium can be seen a bit further on, and the children on the pavement add inter
to the scene. Note the muddy road surface, well marked by the traffic of horse-drawn vehicles. (*Old Barnsl*

The butcher's shop of James Nelson & Sons is just discernible, with its owner or shop assistant at the doorway, perhaps attracted by the photographer. Next door was Ernest Joll's glass and china shop. Both businesses functioned when Florence Copeland was a small girl. The steam-powered vehicle is an unusual sight, contrasting with an approaching horse and cart. Note the typical fly-posters, plastered on the gable of the property on the right of the photograph. (*Old Barnsley*)

Florence Copeland (centre) with her husband, Fred, share a joke with an unknown photographer, Whitsun, Wombwell, *c.* 1950. The lady on the right is Mrs Rose Conser. (*Florence Copeland*)

Although this image is of poor quality, it provides us with a useful glimpse of the Empire Cinema (demolished in 1965) and adjacent shops in about 1957. (*Colin Massingham*)

The ladies of Mount Tabor Chapel are being entertained by some of the gentlemen, at what Florence described to me as a 'Men's Effort', *c.* 1950. Some of the grateful sitters include Mrs Charlotte Robinson, Mrs Edith Fairhurst, Mrs Ella Firth and Mrs Doris Binns. The cheerful 'waiter-onners' include Joe Lingard, Fred Copeland, Russell Firth, Harry Robinson, Joe Rodwell, Mr Fairhurst and Mr Bonser. (*Florence Copeland*)

Mary's Wombwell

My name is Mary Evans and my maiden name was Dunn. I am the aunt of Florence Copeland (see p. 69) and I am ninety-eight years old. I was born at 46 George Street, Wombwell on 2 January 1905 but we soon moved to Ings Road.

My earliest memory is when I started at Park Street Infants School. Mother was so busy that my eldest sister took me. I was rather shy and I remember listening and watching on my first day.

In the streets we played at skipping and hop-scotch and we used to draw on the pavements. We used to peg rugs indoors, on a frame. You had to do some pegging before going out to play. There were no carpets.

During Wombwell Feast week we were on holiday from school. The fair was where the police station is today and also where the Railway pub is. There were cocks and hens and dancing shows; and it was Tuby's fair. I was so fascinated that I lost track of time and Mum and Dad had to come looking for me.

At Whit I went to Low Valley Chapel and also for the anniversary, and took part in the Sings.

Father's name was John William Dunn and Mother was called Hannah. He walked to Wombwell from Staffordshire to seek work in the mines, getting a job at Houghton Main. Mother was left behind to begin with. He had a different dialect to local people. He worked underground when the coal was got by pick and shovel.

I remember the pit strike of 1912. The men used to play football for charity. At the bottom of Station Road there was a big house, and people used to go there 'for relief'.

There was a royal visit in 1912. Queen Mary and King George came and we were taken from the infants' school and placed at the other side of the road, the tall boys and girls at the back and the small ones at the front. We had little flags to wave. I was only tiny, so was at the front, but I was a little disappointed when the Queen passed by – I expected her to be wearing a crown and regalia and not just a hat and coat!

I have special memories of the start of the First World War. My mother took me to Wombwell Town Hall when they announced it from the balcony. There was a big crowd. My two brothers were in the Navy and my father, being impulsive, enlisted, saying that his age was thirty-five but he was really fifty-five. I think they were desperate for recruits. He went to the Dardanelles. I was still at school when there were rowdy peace celebrations.

There were six girls in the family and five boys but Mother had seventeen children in all, several of them dying young. Our terraced house had a 'house' and a scullery. Upstairs was a good-sized landing with a space for a bed. There were also beds in the attic. We slept two at the top of the bed and two at the bottom. Coal was kept in the cellars, and the toilets were outside, a piece of wood with a large and small hole, shared with our neighbour.

Mother washed our clothes every night. There was a mangle and a peggy tub and a tin bath was hung on a nail outside the back door. When we had a bath the water had to be boiled on the fire in pans and kettles. It was a special occasion!

Mary Evans (née Dunn) whose childhood memories of Wombwell stretch back to before the First World War. (South Yorkshire Times)

We never went on holiday, just a club trip or a day trip to the seaside by train. There were also charabanc trips when the ladies had to hold on to their veiled hats. There were Camplejohns, Tommy Lee and Mellors.

When I was about eleven I went to live in Wales, at Wrexham, with my uncle and aunt. I got my first job there when I was fourteen, at the Registrar of Births, Marriage and Deaths. In the 1920s I moved back to Staffordshire and worked at a printers, cleaning the machines and feeding them paper. Eventually I came back to Wombwell in the mid-1920s and got a job at another printers – Cheesman's, on Market Hill, Barnsley. I worked there quite a few years and then at a butcher's shop at Lundwood, then returned to Cheesman's.

Mary Evans and family celebrate the ninetieth birthday of her niece, Florence, at Jump Chapel. Standing, left to right: Sylvia Richardson, Edna Sykes, Mary Evans, Florence Copeland, Caroline and Joanne Hodgson. Seated: Jack and Mildred Collin. (*Florence Copeland*)

A wonderful photograph of Wombwell High Street from the collection of Chris Sharp, probably dating from before 1910. There is an interesting parade of shops on the right-hand side of the road and, across the way, by Marsh Street, the unmistakable Horse Shoe public house. The children attracted by the photographer's presence look smartly dressed, but the woman standing outside the United Counties Bank has a more utilitarian appearance. (*Old Barnsley*)

A Centenarian Looks Back – The Colourful Life and Times of John Bailey

My name is John Bailey but I get called Jack. I was born in Wombwell on 24 December 1900 so am now 102 years old. I had four brothers and four sisters. My mother's maiden name was Doo and she was christened Sarah Ellen but everyone called her Nell. Grandfather, Samuel Dook, wa a farmer near the location of the Station Lane Club and came from Holland. He also had greengrocer's shop, 8 Station Road, opposite Smith Street.

My father, John Bailey, was a miner and worked at most of the local pits but kept getting move on because of his outspoken views. He came from Staffordshire, so had a Black Country accen He called a loaf of bread a round of bread. Mother was very hard-working and very kind.

I can remember living in three houses in Marsh Street, numbers ten, twenty-two and thirty one. There was the 'house' and the kitchen and the backs. The houses were owned by a ma called Marsh who lived at number two. There were just two bedrooms. Four lasses were in on bedroom and five lads in th other. Bathtime was ever Friday and we used the sam water but mother kep heating it up with a kettle or the fire. We had our ear 'syringed' every Frida whether we liked it or not [laughs] Wash day was fiv days a week.

We left Marsh Street to liv at 14 Station Road, opposit the door of the Workin Men's Club and had a shop Mother used to make ice cream and when I was a bo I used to stand there (stal outside shop) from ten in th morning until eleven a night, apart from meals

John Bailey (right) shares a joke with Thurnscoe Male Voice Harmonic Choir conductor and friend Colin Leech, Wombwell, 27 March 2003. (*Brian Elliott*)

selling Bailey's pure ices. We also sold sweets and fruit, it was a general shop. Every Saturda morning I had to go to the railway station and fetch a block of ice which came from Grimsby an had to pull it up the hill to the shop.

When I was only nine, every Friday I used to wash an old man's swollen feet for a penny whicl I took to my mother. I had a lot of jobs as a young lad. Mr and Mrs Drewery had a lock-up sho on High Street [25] opposite the post office. They were agents for someone's sausages and it was sort of delicatessen as well. I worked for them when I was ten. I had to get there at seven on Saturday morning and go to Wolfenden's farm, which was next to the shop, and collect the horse bring it to the front door and help put the goods on the dray, and then I went with the meste right up to Wombwell Main and Hemingfield, calling at houses and shouting 'Drewery's sausage

The old Horse Shoe Hotel, stockist of Whitworth's Wath Beers, situated at the top of Marsh Street. The proprietor, Frank Reeson (wearing bowler and suit), and his staff appear to be outside the main entrance. He may not have been too pleased at the flyposting and graffiti clearly visible. One of the posters relates to Sunday closing, warning men of their rights; the other advertises a series of meetings concerning the Leesing Bill and helps us to date the photograph to 1908 when John Bailey was a boy. The ornate gas lamp is an interesting feature. (*Old Barnsley*)

A rare photograph showing the backs of Marsh Street in the early 1930s, but probably little changed (apart from the fallen wall) from the time when the Bailey family lived there during the early 1900s. (*Colin Massingham*)

and polony'. I had to run back and forwards with orders. I was so tired by the time we got to the Milton Arms at Hemingfield at about half past eleven at night. The mester took goods into the pub and stayed there, drinking, while I was outside, cold and waiting. He came back an hour or so later, drunk, so I had to get the horse home, put it in the stable and feed it. I got 1s wages and my dinner, which was a jug of cocoa and a ham sandwich.

I went to Park Street School. There was a Darfield teacher called Owen and – I must have been clever – he asked me to take the infants every Friday. I was about ten years old. He played the piano and composed a school song [John sings several verses, including]:

God Bless our Park Street School
'Tis there we play our anthem
'Tis there we spend our joyous days
In weather fine or rain.
We raise our voices loud and strong
When joining in that good old song:
God bless our school,
And long may it endure
Free from the throngs of strife
Taking you through the path of truth
And pointing to the path of life.

Boxing matches were held at the Empire and I well remember the Mexborough heavyweight 'Iron' Hague, coming here when he was a budding champion. All us kids followed him and his supporters to the Prince of Wales public house and he threw a handful of pennies to the crowd. I got one but an adult took it from me.

There was a terrible railway accident at Littleworth Lane, near Darfield Main, in 1911. The brakes failed and there was a rare old pile-up. I always had to be up early as I had my father's and all the kid's boots to clean. I was looking out of the back door and I could see the pile-up. I skipped my breakfast and ran to see what had happened. What a smash. The engine was upside down and there was hardly anyone there, apart from myself. I stayed there all day and did not go to school. The accident was shown on the *Pathé Gazette News* in cinemas and I was on it! So I could not deny to the teachers as to where I had been. I got six straps as a result.

I remember the 1912 miners' strike and all the misery it caused to the elderly. I used to go to the Lundhill pit tips, picking coal for home use and for my grandparents. We were like a lot of moles, scratching for bits of coal and also used to dig deep. Sometimes bigger boys used to take over and steal our coal. I coal picked all day and once the pram I used to carry the sack of coal was knocked over by some lads and the coal taken from us.

I left school when I was thirteen and got a job the next day washing bottles at Wombwell glassworks but it was lousy work. I got 3 or 4s a week and was allowed 1d for every shilling. Walking about with 4s in my pocket was a marvellous feeling. I left because all my mates worked at Mitchell's pit top and got 6s a week.

I moved to Houghton Main but had difficulty because of my father's reputation. I was a pony driver and worked at a place called Number Sevens, about 3 miles from the pit bottom. One day

he train smash that John Bailey 'witnessed' took place on 13 December 1911 and was soon seen on a
eries of picture postcards, this example from the camera of Barnsley's George Washington Irving. Sadly, two
nen from the shunting engine were killed despite the courageous efforts of the runaway Sheffield–Wath
oods train driver. (*Brian Elliott*)

here was a roof fall on the main roadway and we were trapped. The deputy got us all together
nd told us that the oldest man, Mr Conway, and the youngest lad, which was me, were to lead
veryone out through the old workings, long abandoned. There was a stream of them following
s, some with no lights and I wondered if we would get out alive. I was crying and very
ightened. Occasionally we would sit down and have a rest. From the front I noticed something in
he distance. It was some help, the rescue team had found us. We could see their lamps a long
ay off. We flashed our lamps and they found us, gave us a blanket each and got us out of the pit.
walked home from the pit to my house at Station Road, then work again the next day.

I soon finished work at Houghton Main. My father did not have a good reputation with the
osses there, so he took me to Mitchell's and pleaded for me to get a job. I did not like it. It was
errible. I came out of the pit and plucked up courage to tell my father that I did not want to go
own again. He was strict and the boss and gave me good hidings, so it took some doing. Mr
ritain, the enginewright at Mitchell's said that I could have a job on the pit top. I knew him
ecause I used to deliver groceries to his house from my grandmother Dook's shop. It probably
elped his decision. Even so, it was a lousy job on the pit top. I was motty-hanging. Each man had
motty, which were for the tubs that were weighed on the pit hill, checked by one from the
niners' union and one from the bosses. There was a great heap of motties and it took me all day

to see to them. I also worked on the screens, a rotten job. The 'bummer' was a chapel man but lousy boss. He was always shouting at us. There was no resting. Eventually I got promoted an worked in the blacksmith's shop as a smith's striker and got proficient with shoeing horses, in fa they used to send for me when he was not there, and I had to go underground to shoe a horse o my own. I soon started making horse shoes myself. On Saturdays I used to have to go to a field Low Valley where some of the ponies were kept and look after them, fasten them up for th horseman to collect and take down the pit. I worked at this job until I got married. Then I went the technical college to study shoeing horses.

I met my late wife, Elsie Thorpe, at a party organised by Stairfoot Chapel. Every Sunday me an two friends used to go to different chapels. I did not see her for a while but I played in th Wombwell Band and when we had an engagement at Ardsley Feast I met her again and arrange to meet her at the Black Bull at Stairfoot, but she did not turn up and I had waited three hours! did not see her for some time until one Sunday when I was stood on the Rabbit Run. Everyon used to walk from Wombwell Empire to the top of Littlefield Lane, back and forth, and we woul pass groups of girls, sometimes passing them twenty times. We hadn't more than a penny in ou pockets. I was on my own when Elsie and her sister walked by and we got talking again. M father arrived and I introduced them to him. We all shook hands and that sealed it! We marrie

An interesting family photograph showing all eleven members of the Bailey family, *c.* 1929. Back row, left right: Vera (aged 18), William, Marcus, Hilda Mary (eldest), Sidney, John (now aged 102) and Barbar Front row: Mrs Mary Ellen Bailey ('Nellie'), Stephen (still in short trousers, worked at Taylor's Printer Wombwell, and later emigrated to New Zealand), Nora (youngest, now aged 88) and Paul Baile (*Derek Bailey*)

t Stairfoot Chapel in 1923. Derek, my oldest on, was born in 1926, at a nursing home up heffield Road.

Wombwell Feast was held where the Working 1en's Club is now, over the canal bridge, and on at side was my grandfather's field and the asworks. The Feast was always split into two, p by the Empire and Athron's farm.

I remember the circus coming to Wombwell, oming to my grandfather's field. I was ightened of the lions. I also remember eroplanes down Broomhill. There was a isplay (Sir John Cobham's Flying Circus) and cost 10s to go up. I couldn't afford it but had go. It was about 1927.

There were meetings in Wombwell Pavilion uring the 1926 miners' strike. A chap called gden was the miners' secretary and he would ay: 'The keynote of this meeting means that ou have to go back to work, otherwise they re having to cut down your wages.' Herbert mith was the miners' president. I heard him peak in Wombwell marketplace, but I was in nsurance then, earning good money, about £3 week. I had worked as an insurance man for bout ten years, after leaving the pit.

I left insurance to be a partner with my rother, Sidney, who had a butcher's shop on ligh Street, but this did not work out and I ound myself without employment for the first me in my life. I had nothing, so I went to the abour Exchange in Barnsley to sign on but ouldn't get any money. I was heartbroken but n the bus on the way home a Labour ouncillor sat by me and we got chatting. le told me that they wanted a rent collector, wo days a week, at Wombwell town hall, for 5s a day. I was so pleased to get the job and oon started work full-time. Eventually I was

John Bailey and Elsie Bailey (née Thorpe) after their wedding in 1924, probably outside 24 Gordon Street, Stairfoot where Elsie lived. John looks the part in his double-breasted dark suit, white shirt and striped tie, though his trousers are a little on the short side . . . but just look at those polished shoes and wavy hair! Elsie looks wonderful in her wedding dress. A royal wedding, the marriage of Princess Mary and Viscount Lascelles in 1922, had a big impact on wedding fashion all over the country. Here the bride is wearing an attractive short (ankle-length) white dress with a long veil, white stockings and shoes. Note the large bouquet. (*Derek Bailey*)

noved to the electricity department and I was there for eleven years. I finished up in charge of an ffice for the workmen.

I got called up at the age of forty-three. I was in the PPW (Publicity and Psychological Warfare) n the Army. We had to drop leaflets, like they are doing now in Iraq. All our officers had been newspaper men. I met Richard Dimbleby who later became the famous television commentator. There were only a small group of us. I also met Field Marshal Montgomery several times. The first occasion was when I was ordered by the colonel to take a bronze head and shoulder of Montgomery, made by a French sculptor, as a gift to the Field Marshal. It was during the battle of Caan. Every 10 yards or so I was stopped and checked. Eventually I got to a big house and the sergeant major took me, with the bust under my arm, to a Captain Clifford who was at the door. After he checked with someone more senior I was taken to see the commander-in-chief himself. He was with about a dozen generals and they were placing hundreds of Christmas cards around the room. They were dressed up in fine uniforms and men were dying nearby. Montgomery must have been pleased as he said, 'Take the corporal for a meal.' Much later I met him again at Badhausen. I got spruced up as I was going to receive a Certificate of Merit. There was a photographer there and I asked him if he wouldn't mind taking a photograph of me being presented with the certificate but the colonel would not allow it. The photographer could only take the back of me. I was at another battle and Montgomery was in his caravan. I went to it and there was a colonel and a brigadier present inside as well. They were playing with two dogs. Montgomery was OK but he was a very strict person and teetotal and expected everyone to be the same. I have been at several meetings of his when he used to say to the troops before he started his speech, 'Now, get your coughing done', so that they would not disturb his monologue.

Until recently I sang in the famous Thurnscoe Harmonic Male Voice Choir, with Colin Leech as our conductor. I have also been a member of Wombwell Mixed Choir and Houghton Main Male Voice Choir.

My secret of a long life? Well, it is to be normal in all things. I never abused my life. I used to have a glass of beer rather than two or more and stopped smoking cigarettes and later stopped smoking a pipe.

Sergeant John Bailey holds a pair of dachshunds, Belgium, c. 1944. (*John & Derek Bailey*)

The commander-in-chief of the British Forces bids goodbye and shakes the hand of Sergeant John Bailey in the Königshof Hotel, Bad Oeynhausen, Germany, Friday morning (10 a.m.), 26 April 1946. (*Derek Bailey*)

Field Marshal Montgomery and some of his senior staff and aides. (*John & Derek Bailey*)

John Bailey, celebrating his 100th birthday by blowing out the candles of one of his cakes, held by his daughter-in-law, Joyce, Christmas Eve, 2000. (*Derek Bailey*)

Three generations of the Bailey family: John (seated), with son Derek and grandson John (of Beech Farm/Beech House Farm, Hemingfield). (*Derek Bailey*)

5

The Rural Scene

Miss Mabel Coulson and Prince, at Home Farm, Billingley,
28 September 1934, 'where we chopped turnips and mixed cattle
food'. Prince was an ex-barge horse converted to farm work.
(*Lynn Bembridge*)

Mabel Crawford (née Coulson, 1913–2002), Remembers Billingley.

Based on an interview recorded on 29 January 2002 and family history material courtesy of Mabel's daughter, Lynn Bembridge who still lives in the village.

Walter Coulson (left) and baby (probably his daughter, Christiana) outside their home, the converted dovecote, Flat Lane. (*Lynn Bembridge*)

I was born at The Crofts (High Street) in Billingley, opposite Beech House, on 29 November 1913. It was a smallholding. There was a 'house' or living room and a downstairs parlour. Upstairs were two bedrooms, a storeplace over the top of the stairs where we put apples in winter. Lighting was by paraffin lamps when I was a girl, also candles and then Tilley lamps which were marvellous. You had to walk about with a lantern with a candle if you went out after dark. We did not have carpets, just matting. We had coal and log fires. The Fitzwilliams of Wentworth owned the property and much of the village. We paid rent twice a year. There was an earth closet. We had an orchard which had every variety of apple tree that you could think of, and also greengage, yellowgage and plum trees. We had a cow place. There were two heifers and three calves. Adjoining the house was the lathe which stood on a stone floor where we mixed the animal food. We also kept pigs, buying a litter and feeding 'em up for pork.

Now, some family history. My mother's name was Emily Atkinson (1873–1951) before she was married. She lived at Pigeon Cote House on Flat Lane, and after her marriage to Walter Coulson (1881–1951), at the family home known as The Crofts, and then at Home Farm (Chapel Lane). I was the youngest of five children: Charles Dannott (b. 1906), Christiana (b. 1907, named from Bunyan's *Pilgrim's Progress*), Ada (b. 1911) and Arthur (b. 1909). My father worked at Beech House, but came to the village from Grasby in Lincolnshire. He used to say he was a 'yellowbelly'! He was a miner and had to come home wearing his mucky pit clothes.

My maternal grandfather, John Atkinson (b. 1842), married Harriet Barber (1843–1913) in 1867. They had six

A modern view of Pigeon Cote House, a handsome, tall brick building probably converted to domestic usage during the mid-nineteenth century. Note the blocked doorways in the gable. The upper one once allowed access into the main chamber of the eighteenth-century dovecote, which would have housed several hundred birds. The young birds or squabs were a valuable source of fresh meat, and their eggs were also used in cooking. (*Brian Elliott*)

eech House (Joseph Haigh's farm), where Walter
oulson worked when he moved to Billingley from
ncolnshire, in the late 1890s. This image is from
postcard sent from Wombwell by 'William' who
ved there in February 1907. (*Brian Elliott*)

alter Coulson (1881–1951) or 'Billingley Bill' as he
as known when he worked at Hickleton Main. He
arried a Billingley girl, Emily Atkinson. From a *carte-de-
site* produced by Joseph Matthews of Louth, Lincolnshire.
ynn Bembridge)

children and lived at The Crofts. Harriet's parents were Joshua Barber (b. 1806) and Harrie⟨t⟩ White (1804–64). They married in 1826 and had ten children, my grandmother, Harriet, bein⟨g⟩ the youngest. Going back even further, Joshua's father was Richard Barber (1767–1822) wh⟨o⟩ married Martha Rook. They lived at The Crofts and were my maternal great-great-grandparent⟨s⟩ so you see, I can trace my Billingley roots back to at least the middle of the eighteenth century.

Mabel Coulson and her cat, in the stackyard of Home Farm, late 1920s. (*Lynn Bembridge*)

One of my earliest memories is ⟨of⟩ walking down the Green towards th⟨e⟩ main road. It was just a lane ther⟨e.⟩ There were wild flowers growing an⟨d⟩ banks of elm trees. I turned along th⟨e⟩ bottom and saw George Henr⟨y⟩ Casson. He took me back home on h⟨is⟩ carrier's wagon. George used to go t⟨o⟩ Doncaster every Tuesday an⟨d⟩ Saturday. You could travel with hi⟨m⟩ or get something delivered. M⟨y⟩ grandmother, after a pig had bee⟨n⟩ killed, used to send everything fro⟨m⟩ sausages and brawn pieces of pork. ⟨It⟩ was like a cart with a top on, like a⟨n⟩ old-fashioned wagon.

I attended the school at Grea⟨t⟩ Houghton, walking there and back⟨.⟩ After that I went to the Girls' Hig⟨h⟩ School (Barnsley) until I was about sixteen. By then the family had moved from The Crofts t⟨o⟩ Home Farm, on Chapel Lane.

We were old-fashioned farmers and had a lot of work to do as the farm had been neglecte⟨d.⟩ Some of the fields had 'onion wicks', like twitch grass, growing. Well, we spent days gettin⟨g⟩ them out and burning them, but finished up with some good land. We had about 67 acres an⟨d⟩ the land that belonged to the smallholding. It was a mixed farm, with cattle and pigs: and I ha⟨d⟩ a goat. I worked with horses, a little bit of ploughing but mainly harrowing, dragging an⟨d⟩ weeding. Often my brother ploughed with the horse and I followed on the presser. It made ⟨a⟩ ridge or groove so that rows of corn could grow. The horses names that I remember wer⟨e⟩ Bounce, Polly and her foal, Bounce. When it was early summer we were up at four and worke⟨d⟩ until it got too hot, then had a rest in the afternoon. We then went back and worked until th⟨e⟩ evening. We always managed to get home for our meals. Sometimes, say when we wer⟨e⟩ stooking, putting all the sheaves together to dry, we had dinner brought out to us in the field⟨s.⟩ When it was harvest time and May time farmers used to get a barrel of beer in, but we used t⟨o⟩ drink a lot of lemonade, made with hot water poured on crystals, or maybe a desert spoon ⟨of⟩ oatmeal was put in a bottle of water.

I remember some of the names of the fields at Home Farm. There was Top, Middle and Botto⟨m⟩ Harthills. Further on there was the Top, Middle and Bottom Rushes. Then there was Big and Littl⟨e⟩ Flatts; also near Green and Far Green. We also farmed a field down at Broomhill. It was dam⟨p⟩

alter Coulson continued to keep a
nallholding as well as working as a miner.
ere he is, with daughter Mabel, by the gate
the stackyard of Home Farm, probably on
e same day as the photograph shown
pposite. (*Lynn Bembridge*)

Mabel Coulson with Polly at Home Farm,
c. 1927. The stables can be seen in the
background. (*Lynn Bembridge*)

down there. I think they called it the Ings. We cut the corn with scythes and used a taking-u
rake which had a long handle and three prongs. You brought enough corn to your foot and mad
a band round with corn, twisting the strands until we made a sheath.

I started attending the Sunday School at the chapel when I was three and I'm still going to th
chapel. At Whit the lads pulled a cart carrying an organ and we went round Middlecliffe, Littl
Houghton and the village singing anniversary hymns and collecting; and in the afternoon ther
was tea.

There used to be Billingley Feast for our entertainment. There was a tennis court and I playe
tennis, but there weren't any dances. There was a farmers' dance at Clayton. We would wal
there, dance all night and walk home for two o'clock in the morning!

How did I meet my husband? Well, I was taking the cows back to the field and he was walkin
to Goldthorpe, and it was as simple as that. He must have spotted me! We went to the pictures i
Goldthorpe. I was courting about a year. George or 'Juddy' was from Little Houghton. He worke
on the coke ovens at the pit but had just come out of the Army. We were married at Hemswort
Register office on 25 July 1935. We lived with his mother for a little while until we got a propert
first a cottage in Middlecliffe and then in Billingley (now Waldron's) on Chapel Lane.

There was a shop in the village, Ashwood's, which sold just about everything, candles, paraffi
sweets and so on. There were quite a few wells in gardens and then there was the town wel
originally in Well Lane, but later in Finney's, Chapel Lane. Then there was the village pond. The
used to bring horses and drays through a flagged part so that they could wash their feet an
clean the wheels. There was also a village pinfold where stray farm animals were onc
impounded.

Taking a rest from preparing the land at Billingley in the twenties. The men included in this evocative stud
by the Wombwell photographer R.J. Short are, left to right, Charles Coulson, Arthur Coulson, -?- and J
Philips (from Highgate). (*Lynn Bembridge*)

ome Farm,
illingley, 1920s.
he war memorial
an be seen in the
reground, at the
nction with
hapel Lane. The
ttle girl at the
edroom window
as Mabel
oulson.
ynn Bembridge)

Children gather by
the side of Billingley
village pond on a
Saturday morning
in the early 1920s.
Mabel Coulson
(centre) is wearing a
white ribbon in her
hair, and sisters Ada
and Christiana are
standing behind her.
(*Lynn Bembridge*)

he memorial, Home Farm, at
he centre of the attractive
illage of Billingley, 2000.
Brian Elliott)

Mabel Crawford (née Coulson), pictured in her Billingley home on 29 January 2002. (*Brian Elliott*)

Mabel Crawford continued to lead an active life well into her late eighties. Here she is, in 2002, opening the Billingley Jubilee celebrations. Mabel's death, on Saturday 20 July 2002, was received with great sadness by her family, friends and neighbours. Her funeral was held in Billingley chapel, where she had worshipped since the age of three. (*Lynn Bembridge*)

Arthur Coulson (1909–87) – a Well-Loved Village Character Remembers

Arthur was the brother of Mabel Coulson, information courtesy of Lynn Bembridge

When I got to fourteen my dad said, 'I'm going to take thee to Doncaster Hirings and hire thee out for a year and a day and get paid once a year.' I got a bob pocket money off him and I would get £15 a year there. I was hired to Mr Booth of Manor Farm, Wrangbrook. We were up at half-past four in a morning – with horses stood at the back of the hedge until it got daylight so you could go up the field. We had to stop there until half past five at night. When it got to Saturday at noon, t' job stood as we were finishing. You had Saturday afternoon off and Sunday. We went to Upton chapel on Sunday.

When we had breakfast we had a lump of fat bacon apiece, there were four of us. When we got home at twelve they made us a rice pudding made with water and plenty of it, and there was a 2 lb jar of treacle to put on the pudding.

When I got a bit older I got a job at Kirk Smeaton. That was a good place. We always got 6 lb of corned beef in a block. My mother, Emily Coulson (née Atkinson), was a good cook and could make a good meat and potato pie with a crust 2 inches thick. She would make a hole in the top to pour water from the kettle into it, then she'd cut it up; and when there were seven of us there wasn't much left. She made it in a big bowl. If there was any left we would have it for supper.

Mother had a great big iron saucepan which would hold 2½ gallons of water. She used to put a ham bone in, an old hen, turnips, carrots and lentils; then she used to make fourteen dumplings and they floated on the top.

Walter Coulson, ready for work on the farm. He was one of the great characters of Billingley. (*Lynn Bembridge*)

Colin Leech Remembers Great Houghton and his musical childhood in the 1930s and '40s

I was born at 26 Springfield Road, a small two-bedroomed terraced house, then also known a Well Lane, on 9 January 1934. When I was about two years old we moved to a three-bedroome council house at 9 Rotherham Road, Sandhill. I was one of six children. Helen ('Nellie'), my eldes sister, stayed at home, and the two next in line (Irene or 'Rene' and Gladys) went into service. M youngest sister was named Nancy. My older brother, Jack, spent most of his childhood with m paternal grandparents as our terraced house was on the small side.

My father, John Willie, worked from the age of thirteen as a miner a Houghton Main, but soon moved on t Dearne Valley pit [and was there] unt his retirement at the age of sixty-eigh He was born in the village. He joined th Yorkshire & Lancashire Regiment an was at the Somme, also at Ypres, one the lucky ones who survived the Grea War. When I was nine or ten he took m down the pit, and he used to tell me tha whatever I did when I grew up, I mus not go down any mines to work. Ther was nothing there, he would say, othe than hard work and dust. He worked i dreadful conditions. I've known him com home and be absolutely soaking wet. O some days, though, he used to get t work early so that he could earn a littl extra money by filling a tub on th surface. Times were very hard. Mothe took in washing and did chores fo people, anything to earn a little money My paternal grandfather, Samuel migrated to Great Houghton as a youn single man, from Ireland, in the 1870s They were sinking pits in our area ther He became a pit deputy. The only tim that Helen, his wife, left the village wa when she walked to Wentworth once o

Colin Leech, aged two and a half, as 'England's Last Hope', Great Houghton village fair, 1936. Young Colin won the fancy-dress competition. (*Colin Leech*)

twice a year to pay her rent. They rented their old cottage, just behind the Methodist chapel, from the Fitzwilliams.

Most of the children in the village attended Sunday schools which were, along with th working men's clubs, centres of most social activities. It was at Sunday school that my lifelon love of music started, when we began rehearsing for the anniversary. Reg Taylor and his wif

Colin Leech, the 'Boy Soprano', and some of his medals and awards. It must have been quite something for the small village of Great Houghton to have one of its schoolboys on national radio. (*Colin Leech/Dentons of Barnsley*)

Clara were choirmaster and organist, respectively, and did much to encourage me. They must have recognised some potential, suggesting that I should benefit from tuition. I went to Miss Cathy Noble at Thurnscoe for singing lessons, a lovely lady who was wonderful with children. She did so much to encourage music in Thurnscoe and Great Houghton. It wasn't long before doors opened for me to progress to radio broadcasts on programmes such as *Children's Hour*, *Workers' Playtime* and *Works Wonders*. Since those childhood days I have always been involved in some form of music-making.

I attended Sandhill Infant and Junior Schools. I remember the start of the Second World War when a classmate called Bob Copping said to me in the playground, 'This a war started today' and I asked him what a war was. He told me, 'It's when they all feight'. The headmaster was Mr Sanders and my first teacher was Miss Doris Hanson, one of the nicest ladies that I have ever met. In those days we had a nap in the afternoon in a small field near the classroom. The war seemed a long way off, but we could hear Sheffield being bombed and could see the flashes of explosions and the barrage balloons. We had to carry gas masks all the time. Rationing was introduced and we had to have cod liver oil every day, from a three-sided bottle, all of us using the same spoon! Fruit was a luxury, but a box used to arrive at school once or twice a year and we were treated to half an apple.

Sandhill then and now. The old photograph above dates from the early 1900s. A few men are playing an impromptu game of cricket on the playing field, still dressed in formal clothes. Note the steps leading up to the terraced properties on Turner Street (A), the 'bottom' working men's club (B), Mrs Clarkson's corner shop (C) and Brookes' newsagent's (D) facing each other across New Street, Kitchen's corner shop (E) at the end of Edward Street and Hepworth's fish and chip shop (F). Colin recalls that as a boy he used to sit on a three-legged stool and sing in the fish shop, providing live entertainment for Mr Hepworth's customers. The two vehicles would now be classed as of veteran status. Maybe that's the photographer's bicycle leant on the bridge wall. The modern view helps us to appreciate the changes that have occurred to this area over the last hundred years. (*Old Barnsley/Brian Elliott*)

I started to get noticed when I sang at music festivals and in competitions and used to get invited to sing in public. Eventually I was invited to sing on the BBC's *Children's Hour* radio programme. I was taken to Piccadilly in Manchester for the programmes which were broadcast live. Violet Carson (who later played Ena Sharples in *Coronation Street*) was the pianist. I sang solo, accompanied by Violet, standing in front of a big microphone suspended from the ceiling on springs. I was invited back several times and I guess that locally I became quite well known. The early recordings were made at the end of the war. For *Works Wonders* a car picked me up from school. The programme was broadcast from the Co-op.

The wireless was a very popular home entertainment, but you had to collect the heavy batteries for recharging on a regular basis. The houses were gas-lit until after the end of the war.

The Old Hall was a very fine building but was sadly demolished. It stood near to the Co-op and used to have wrought-iron gates at each end of its driveway. The Old Crown public house was also a historic building but had been demolished. There was also a railway station in Great Houghton and a regular service between Adlington and Wakefield. We nicknamed the familiar engine and one carriage 'The Titanic'.

Everyone knew everyone else in the village. There were many local characters. One of them was the barber, Sid Clarke. He seemed to know everything about everybody and would recount stories about the village for hours. Most

Colin Leech in his Darfield home, 4 February 2003. Though retired, Colin continues to have a very active interest in music. He is conductor of no fewer than four choirs: Wombwell Mixed, Thurnscoe Harmonic Male Voice, Horbury Ladies and Retford. (*Brian Elliott*)

of the shopping was done at the Co-op where the 'divi' came in very handy for those little extras.

I left Sandhill School at the age of eleven and for a few months went to Darfield Foulstone School and then on to Wath Grammar. After I left the grammar school I got an apprenticeship as a decorator at the Co-op until getting called up for National Service. Later, after getting married, I started my own decorating business in Darfield in premises I called The Paint Shop, working there until I retired.

An interesting early photograph of Great Houghton Co-op and the Old Hall when it functioned as a public house. A small group of patrons appears to have assembled just outside the ancient hall. Colin recalls Mr Kirk as the Co-op shop manager during the war and, like many other former customers, still remembers his dividend number: 3355, a vital piece of information to be given at every transaction. (*Old Barnsley*)

The Old Hall was a substantial Elizabethan mansion long associated with the Rodes family, staunch nonconformists. This fine building was demolished in about 1960, following a serious fire. Fortunately the Jacobean chapel still survives and is still in use for services. One Darfield resident, whose grandparents, the Welfords, had the pub in the 1920s, was able to recall the upstairs rooms which had wide floor boards and a gallery with rooms leading off. It had a dark blue fitted carpet and there were blue velvet curtains to the windows. A bed was described as 'of a lovely golden coloured wood and very highly polished'; and next to it was a small desk, above which was a picture of a cavalier. A Great Houghton resident, Mrs Dorothy Higginbottom, whose uncle was landlord at the time of the fire, informed me of the great affection she had for the splendid building and its contents. (*Margaret Mann*)

Some people with Great Houghton connections may recognise themselves or family and neighbours assembled for this royal celebration, possibly marking the coronation of George VI in 1937. (*Old Barnsley*)

Another interesting early view of Sandhills, taken this time from the village. On the right we can see the entrance to Edward Street and Kitchen's corner shop. Part of the attractive countryside surrounding Great Houghton is also apparent. (*Old Barnsley*)

Great Houghton Football
Club (First XI) assemble in
front of the Old Hall for a
team photograph, 1908.
Back row, left to right:
F. Leech, J.S. Elliott
(goalkeeper) and W. Shaw.
Middle row: W. Collins,
T. Bladen, T. Jacques, H.
Creighton, J. Walker, W.
Fawcett (secretary) and
T. Immisson. Front row: W.
Harrop (assistant secretary),
O. Walker, J. Moorhouse, W.
Taylor, R. Wrigley, W. Smith.
(*Dorothy Higginbottom*)

A small group of people provides interest for the camera of an unknown photographer who had chosen th
Edward Street shop of John Kitchen as his subject for a picture postcard. Part of the scene can be seen toda
but the shop has long ceased to provide any goods or services and satellite dishes 'decorate' the stone terrac
row. (*Brian Elliott*)

he boulevard-like road that cuts through Great Houghton village attracted the interest of a local hotographer in this inter-war view. One of George White's omnibuses can be seen disappearing in the stance, opposite the Old Hall. Nowadays motorists have to negotiate a long series of traffic-calming 'road imps' whenever passing through the village. (*Old Barnsley*)

other between-the-wars photograph, on this occasion showing a variety of stone properties, both sidential and commercial, along High Street. (*Old Barnsley*)

Sleeve notes from the LP *Stars on Sunday by Request*, including reference to the contribution of Thurnscoe Harmonic Male Voice Choir. Great Houghton's Colin Leech was the choir conductor and choral advisor to the popular Yorkshire Television production that commissioned the record. Colin recalled the recording of two tracks and the thrill of being a part of a project that included such internationally famous names as Bing Crosby and Jimmy Stewart who performed a reading. Mr Stewart had recently lost his son in the Vietnam War and it was Bing Crosby's last recording before his death. (*Courtesy of Yorkshire Television*)

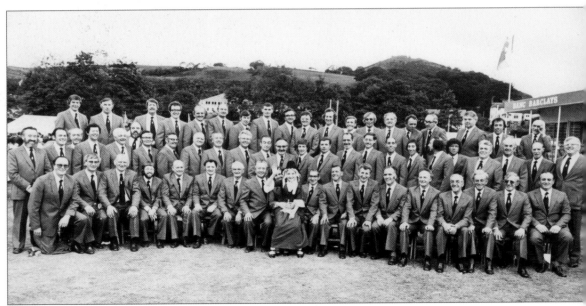

Thurnscoe Harmonic Male Voice Choir has been successful in many national and international competitions over the years. Here, it is at the 1980 International Eisteddfod when the choir achieved a very commendable second prize. Conductor Colin Leech can be seen, standing, on the extreme left of the group. (*Sheffield Newspapers Ltd*)

6

Charabancs
& Omnibuses

A Camplejohn charabanc outside the Golden Ball Hotel, Worksop, with its party of Barnsley Football Club supporters, 3 April 1912. The Tykes played Swindon Town at Notts County's Meadow Lane ground, in a semi-final replay of the English Cup, winning 1–0 thanks to a goal by Bill Bratley. Barnsley went on to win the Cup at Bramall Lane. This impressive vehicle is a 1908 Durham Churchill. Twenty-three-year-old Colin Camplejohn is the driver, with younger brother Sidney (aged eighteen), sitting at the front near side. (*Camplejohn Family Archive*)

The Camplejohns – some Notes and Memories

Courtesy of Barbara Sanders (née Camplejohn)

There have been many ways of spelling the family name, but the most common was Campleshon in the seventeenth century and, from the eighteenth century, Camplejohn. The name may come from the Old English word 'campa', meaning a warrior or camp, a battle. Champion was possibly the first version of the name and a substantial number of Champions lived around Seamer, Cleveland, in the sixteenth century. It perhaps meant 'fighting John' but current thinking is that many surnames have locative origins, and Compiègne in France, or Hambleton in Yorkshire have been suggested as possible sources.

In the early eighteenth century a Miles Camplejohn appeared in Riccall, in the East Riding of Yorkshire, and founded the dynasty from which it seems that all the present-day family are descended. He was a tailor and may have been related to the Camplejohns of Dunnington who were also tailors.

William Camplejohn, great-great-grandson of Miles, was born at Riccall in 1827. He was a wheelwright and carpenter by trade and had worked as a ships' carpenter before finding work on the island of Alderney. William moved to Alderney with his second wife, Elizabeth Dowson, in the early 1860s. Five of their nine children were born there, including my father, Walter (1868–1945). When, after twelve years, work ran out on Alderney, William returned to Yorkshire, and was employed as a carpenter at Darfield Main colliery.

The Camplejohn Brothers firm was started by Walter and his younger brother Septimus Camplejohn (1871-1954). Their first vehicle may have been operational as early as 1904 and certainly by 1905 probably the earliest mechanical public-service vehicle in South Yorkshire. Both brothers started work down the pit but then established a cycle shop in Snape Hill. Thomas Septimus described himself as as a shopkeeper as early as 1899 in the Darfield parish register. My father, Walter, worked as an engine winder at Darfield Main and is described as such in the 1891 census. He remained there until after the First World War when he passed on his job to his nephew, Roy Camplejohn. The Camplejohn Brothers ran charabancs and, later, service buses from Thurnscoe to Barnsley, and also excursions. In 1915 the original partnership broke up when Septimus moved to Bentley, near Doncaster, and set up his own bus company there. Another brother, Anthony Camplejohn (1865–1938), then became a partner. Walter retired as the manager of Camplejohn Brothers in 1928 and his nephew, Colin (1889–1975), took over the day-to-day running of the business. He lived at the office, Alderney Cottages, Low Valley. My father lived at Prospect House at the top of Snape Hill until 1928. Colin continued as manager until 1936 when Sidney Camplejohn (Father's nephew and fourth son of Anthony) was appointed to run the business. Sidney was devoted to the firm and a superb chap. When it was freezing he used to get up several times during the night to run the engines of the buses so that they would start in the morning. Punctuality and reliability were Camplejohn's watchwords. Drivers hated leaving anyone behind and have often heard conductresses cry 'breathe in' so as to pack on another body. The 'no more than eight standing' rule was largely ignored by private operators.

Camplejohn Brothers was a real old 'family' firm. If a driver or conductor was needed in an emergency some family member could be called upon. Anthony, Amos, Sidney, Irvine and Colin were regular drivers. Father had over thirty nephews and nieces living locally and everyone, even sometimes complete strangers, called him 'Uncle Walter'. John William (1890–1963, William Dowson Camplejohn's son) used to leave the shop (now Darfield Museum & Heritage Centre) and travel t

Guildford and other locations to collect buses. Jim Stringfellow, who married Rhoda Camplejohn, and Jack Jepson (married to Jessie Camplejohn) were other drivers. Stanley Wall, whose mother was Ada Camplejohn, worked as a lorry driver with Darfield Motor Co. but also drove buses.

The Camplejohn women were very much involved in the business. My father's first wife, Alice, used to rout the drivers out of their beds to get them off on excursions and even interrupted John William's honeymoon to get him on the road. Sidney's wife, Sarah, was a tremendous help to him and their daughter, Dorothy, worked as a conductress, together with her cousin, Donna Dodson. Mother did all the secretarial work for my father and all the worrying. I remember one incident in about 1936 when plans were being forwarded for a new central bus station in Barnsley. Before the scheme could go ahead all the bus operators had to agree to use the new bus station in place of stands they already had. All agreed apart from my father who had discovered that there was to be a staff canteen and rest room, but for the exclusive use of Yorkshire Traction employees. He told them that he would not agree to the project unless his staff could use the canteen and rest room too. The eventual outcome was that Camplejohn drivers and conductors were allowed to use the new facilities.

My father's idea of 'retirement' was to buy an acre or so of land at the junction of Cat Hill and Doncaster Road and erect a house and garage there in 1927–8, and start a new business under the name of The Darfield Motor Co. The house was 'Tudoresque' in style and had quite expensive features, but no central heating. An Italian was brought in to lay the Tudor Rose mosaic floor in the entrance hall and there were oak gates, doors and panelling and armorial-style stained-glass windows on the landing. It was an exposed spot, so the house could be cold in winter. The house was demolished in 1996 to make way for road improvements. The garage, which still stands, has two floors. The top floor was used as a showroom for servicing cars and lorries and the lower floor housed the two lorries used for the haulage business. We had contracts to lead bricks from brickyards, and in the season, the lorry drivers went to Lincolnshire for weeks on end to lead sugar beet. The lorries worked through the night in the winter, gritting the roads. We were Ford agents and sold and serviced cars. Employees include Alec Clarney, Eric Lackey, Jack Butcher, Stanley Wall and a very reliable engineer, Alan Hopcroft. Mr Scott manned the petrol pumps.

My father had ecologically correct ideas long before there were fashionable. The rainwater from the house and garage was drained into large underground sumps and pumped out in periods of drought, for watering the garden. We had septic tank drainage and, because the mains electricity would have cost £120, an immense sum in those days, my father installed a Petters generator which was run for a few hours a week and charged up with batteries kept in the battery room in the garage. This provided us with a 110 volt electricity supply. The Petters engine had only to cough for my father to hear it and he would stop whatever he was doing to rush to its side. Unlike the house, the greenhouse had underfloor heating. One lit a fire at one end and there was a flue which ran all the way underneath it. The fire was fuelled by open-cast coal which we dug out from an exposed seam behind the garage. There was an arbour at the bottom of the garden with a seat adapted from one of the old charas and the arbour roof and garden rose arches were made out of the ash hoops, also from the charas.

My father died in 1945 and mother sold The Darfield Motor Co., moving to Birmingham in 1951. She remained a partner in Camplejohn Brothers until it was sold to Yorkshire Traction ten years later. Camplejohn's haulage business continued to operate for many more years from Low Valley, owned and managed by Sidney and his family.

The first: this 1905 Arrol Johnson sixteen-seater was delivered to Camplejohns on Good Friday 1906, from works at Paisley, Scotland, and cost around £400. It must have caused a sensation when it appeared in the mining community at Snape Hill, and must have turned heads when en route to Wombwell and on picnic/seaside trips. The driver is James William Camplejohn and sitting with him is either Walter or Thomas Septimus, co-founders of the business. Sitting

behind the driver is James Camplejohn, J.W.'s father, who was chief engineer at Darfield Main for over forty years. To start the engine, a loose handle was used at the side of the vehicle, the action described as 'like turning a mangle'. Interesting features include the handbrake wheel at the driver's right hand, paraffin oil lamps, solid tyres and curtains which could be drawn in adverse weather – and there was no windscreen, though the maximum speed was 12 mph. The intrepid passengers boarded via a folding step down each side of the vehicle. (*Camplejohn Family/Dennis Camplejohn*)

After the pioneering Camplejohns, the next local charabanc owner was Martin Stenton, seen here in an early photograph. Mr Stenton obtained a vehicle known as 'The Up to Date'. Barbara Sanders recalled that Martin was a friend of her father, Walter Camplejohn, and often came to Sunday dinner. He wore a frock coat during the 1930s, and taught Barbara to say, 'I must not play on Sundays, for it would be a sin. Tomorrow is Monday and then may I begin.' (*Barbara Sanders*)

This chara was purchased from a Barnsley publican after a fire. The Camplejohns had it rebuilt at their Snape Hill garage and rebodied at Selby. It is seen on Sheffield Road, Barnsley, *c.* 1912. The usual driver was Billy Camplejohn who later ran the Beer-off, at 2 Vicar Road (now the village museum). (*Camplejohn Family*)

Here we can see a young Sidney Camplejohn at the wheel of a six-door-long charabanc, just after the First World War. The Karrier had a new (1918) chassis but a 1913 body, the previous chassis having been commandeered during the war. The passengers consist of a formidable party of (mainly) ladies, no doubt set on a day out, and suitably dressed for the occasion. (*Camplejohn Family*)

Matlock Bath was a popular Edwardian tourist resort, though it would have taken several hours to get there by road from Darfield/Wombwell. A Camplejohn charabanc pauses outside the Hodgkinson Hotel, South Parade, in 1913. The vehicle is a Durham Churchill, made in Sheffield in 1907/8, capable of seating thirty passengers. The party are officials and wives of Mitchell Main colliery. The VIP group included the pit manager, Joshua Beardshall, undermanager Mr W. Thompson (wearing the silk hat), surveyor Alec Dallas and deputies George Dixon, Alf Walker, Walter Tingle (ice-cream maker) and Ben Sharratt. The confident-looking young driver is Sidney Camplejohn who would soon be in France, driving ambulances during the First World War. When the party arrived back in Wombwell after braving the dusty Derbyshire roads, Sidney said everyone looked as if they had visited a flour mill! (*Camplejohn Family*)

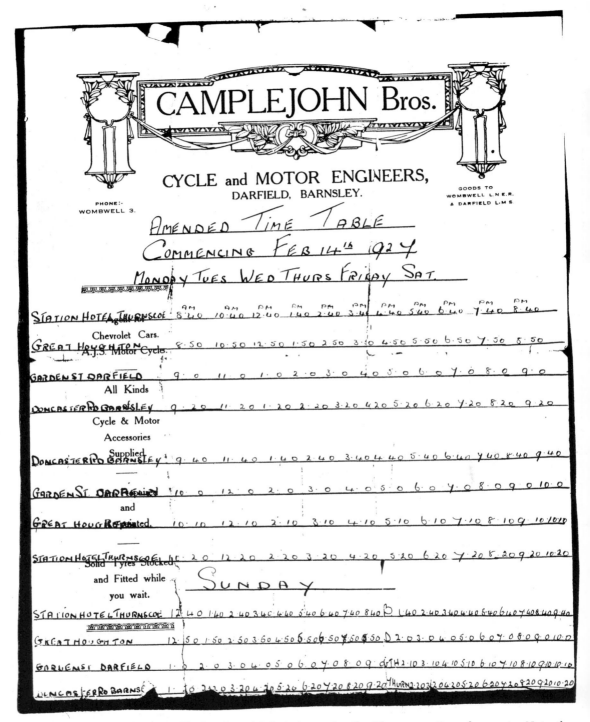

A handwritten weekly timetable for Camplejohn's buses for the Thurnscoe–Barnsley route. Note the telephone number of just one digit: Wombwell 3. (*Barbara Sanders*)

Above: The house and garage at Cat Hill, built by Walter Camplejohn, *c.* 1927. (*Barbara Sanders*)

Left: The Tudor-style house at Cat Hill, with its leaded windows, was quite an imposing landmark on this exposed site. (*Barbara Sanders*)

Below: Further and faster – an example of the Darfield Motor Co.'s flair for advertising can be seen in the rare survival of a match book produced by the British Pullmatch Co. (*Barbara Sanders*)

Tom Lee and Son's Wombwell charabancs and touring cars. The grandest vehicle has luxurious upholstered seats and we also get a good view of the expandable protective hood, very handy in bad weather. Garages had to be of considerable size to house several of these vehicles. (*Malcolm Hambleton*)

After the First World War pneumatic tyres were introduced and there were tremendous changes in the design and performance of public service motor vehicles. Here we can see a Camplejohn Bros coach, registration YG 750, from about 1932. There were always ingenious solutions to customer requirements: the luggage rack on the top of the vehicle was reached from the rear by a folding iron ladder. (*Camplejohn Family*)

amplejohn's always moved
ith the times, as can be seen
 this stylish Dennis bus (Fleet
. 26) parked at Pitt Street,
w Valley, the Mission church
 the background, c. 1948. The
mber eleven placed in the
ont window suggests a recent
 forthcoming excursion.
Robert Mack)

Camplejohn's fleet no. 29
bus, a Sentinel, at
Barnsley bus station,
c. 1957. (Robert Mack)

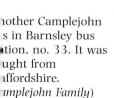

nother Camplejohn
s in Barnsley bus
tion, no. 33. It was
ught from
affordshire.
amplejohn Family)

Camplejohn's 'Blackpool Express' (no. 20) gets ready for one of the first postwar seaside excursions, much appreciated by the happy Darfield passengers, in 1947. This thirty-five-seater vehicle had a Dennis Year body and developed gearbox problems because of a manufacturing fault. Dennis Camplejohn recalled the the body builders had not left sufficient room for the gear lever to travel in the floor. (*Camplejohn Family*)

One of four Sentinel service buses owned b Camplejohn's in the 1950s. They were, according to Sidney's note on the back of the photograph, forty-four seaters and made in Shrewsbury. Dennis Camplejohn adds that the photograph dates from about 1953, taken at the 'top of Darfield', on Barnsley Road. The driver is Dick Cousins and the conductress Anita Beaumont.
(*Camplejohn Family*)

Dennis Camplejohn and bus no. 27, probably at Scarborough, in 1957. Dennis is the son of Sidney Camplejohn who christened him after the famous motor commercial vehicle manufacturer. He was chief mechanic at the Camplejohn garage. (*Dennis Camplejohn*)

Two Camplejohn bus tickets. It's remarkable that such pieces of ephemera have survived.

EXCHANGE

CAMPLEJOHN BROS. DARFIELD Nr. BARNSLEY

Motor Coach Proprietors & Haulage Contractors

THIS EXCHANGE TICKET must be put so as to show amount of ORIGINAL FARE PAID and is issued subject to the Regulations of the Firm as printed in the Firm's Official Time Table. PASSENGER SHOULD NOTE PRICE REMAINING ON TICKET.

"Willebrew" System, Patents 321939 & 567262 — Williamson, Ticket Printer, Ashton-under-Lyne.

TEL.: WOMBWELL 2103

3d
4d
5d
6d
7d
8d
9d
10d
11d
1/-
1/1
1/2
1/3
1/4
1/5
1/6
1/6

7305

V

CAMPLEJOHN BROS. **BLACKPOOL WEEKLY SERVICE**

MOTOR COACH PROPRIETORS

DARFIELD, Nr. BARNSLEY

Tel.: WOMSWELL 2103

"Willebrew" System Patents 321939 & 567262 — Williamson, Ticket Printer, Ashton-under-Lyne.

FROM LAST SATURDAY IN JUNE TO LAST SATURDAY IN SEPTEMBER. **BOOK EARLY.**

NOT TRANSFERABLE. Must be retained for inspection. Issued subject to Firm's regulations. Only valid for travel when shipped in the stage number as which passenger boarded the bus.

8353

1/-	1/-	11d	10d	9d	8d	7d	6d	5d	4d	3½d	3d	2½d	2d	1½d	1d	W/C OUT

SINGLE

Sidney Camplejohn died at the age of ninety-six in 1990. Much of his life was concerned with motor transport: he was an early charabanc driver, mechanic, ambulance driver in the First World War and private omnibus proprietor. After leaving George Street School, Low Valley, he started work, at the age of thirteen, at Dearne Valley colliery, leaving two years later to work at Darfield Main. He was seventeen years old when his extraordinarily long and remarkable career with public service vehicles began. In the 1950s his public service continued when he was elected to Darfield UDC as an independent and he was a founder member of Wombwell Rotary Club. Although I never met Sidney, it is clear from his writings that he had a keen sense of humour and, along with his extensive family, his contribution to the history of transport in South Yorkshire has been enormous. (*Peggy Shaw*)

Many Wombwell and Darfield people will remember T. Burrows & Sons, motor omnibus proprietors, which operated from Melville Street and High Street, Wombwell from the 1920s. Here we can see a Burrows bus with its distinctive number plate, WE 777, in about 1928. The driver is Robert Weston and the conductor, Mr T. Parker. (*Zena Hudson*)

trio of Camplejohn buses, Dennis Lancets, on parade, probably at Middlewood, *c.* 1957. (*Camplejohn amily*)

eat Houghton's omnibus proprietor was George White who is listed in a 1936 directory, but almost rtainly operated for several years earlier. Here we can see a White's (no. 5) bus, WX 3855, parked on a ry quiet Rotherham Road, Great Houghton, during the inter-war period. The unknown school boys sitting the wall add interest to the scene. Note the old school sign. (*Old Barnsley*)

Members of Darfield & Low Valley/Snape Hill WMC look very cheerful before they embark on a bus (Pickersgill's?) trip to London in the 1950s. Those identified by Geoff Harrison of Garden Street, Darfield include Bill Marsden, Alf Wake, Ernest Wake, James Dunn, Simeon Dunn, Simon Dunn, George Gibbs, Tommy Mullins and Colin Corton. (*Bill Marsden/Geoff Harrison*)

This may bring back a few memories: waiting for a bus in old Barnsley bus station, 1960s. We have a good view of Platform A and Haigh's 'threepenny-bit' newsagent's kiosk, always a popular meeting place. (*H. Copley*)

7

Glimpses from Family Albums

A delightful photograph from Kenneth Blackburn's
Wombwell studio of Olwyn Newsome (now Mrs
Olwyn Beard who lives in Hampshire) and her
younger brothers Eric (centre, born 1940, now
resident in France) and Leslie (1944–94), *c.* 1947.
(*Julie Little/Olwyn Beard*)

Many Wombwell people will remember with affection Thomas Arthur Newsome (1890–1966) who was Mayor of Wombwell in the early 1950s. He lived at 32 Snowden Terrace and married Clare Annie Oakley. Newsome Avenue was named in his honour. (*Julie Little/Olwyn Beard*)

The Wombwell wedding of Edna Newsome and Ivy Webb, *c.* 1935. Others in the group are Thomas and Edgar Newsome, George Smith and Phylis Newsome, and William, Horace and Eva Webb. Note the frills on the bridesmaids' dresses and the boy attendant's white suit. By this time wedding dresses had assumed a special significance, one-offs for that special occasion. (*Julie Little/Olwyn Beard*)

The wedding of Herbert Newsome and Eva Webb, *c.* 1940. It is a slightly less formal wedding group than the one above, with the bride and groom seated, flanked by the respective mothers in the party. Eva's veil is much longer than her sister-in-law's. Back row, left to right: Marion Newsome (sister of groom, later Mrs Stables), Joe Newsome (groom's brother), another brother, William Webb (bride's father), Horace Webb (brother of bride) and his wife, Jessie. Front row: Alice (mother of groom), Herbert Newsome (groom), Eva Newsome (bride), Lillian Webb and the small bridesmaid is Olwyn Newsome (now Beard, niece of the bride). (*Julie Little/Olwyn Beard*)

This interesting Edwardian wedding party dates from about 1905, and is believed to have been photographed outside 215 Barnsley Road, Wombwell. The occasion was the marriage of Alfred and Clara Robinson, who, seated, are at the front and centre of the group. The gentlemen look extremely smart in dark lounge suits, wearing boaters or bowler hats, and the women's headwear looks absolutely splendid as do the magnificent bouquets. One elderly lady, probably a widow, appears to be wearing a black ostrich feather atop her hat. In a few years' time ladies' hats became even larger and more flamboyant. (*Malcolm Robinson*)

Esther aged twenty, 1935. (*Esther Johnson*)

Esther Johnson Recalls Aspects of her Early Life

I was born on 24 January 1915 in my mother's (Anne Weigh, b. 1875) shop at the bottom of Pinfold Lane. My maternal grandfather, George Jackson (1836–1903) was a master miller and farmer in Barnsley. When he died in 1903 my grandmother (Esther Ann) my mother and my uncle came to Darfield and ran the shop. Father Albert Edward Weigh, came from Wales to Lancashire and then Yorkshire, finding employment at Darfield Main as a night banksman and met Mum. They married in 1912 and moved to a fairly new house at 36 Vicar Road. He was a diabetic and died in 1924 when I was only nine.

I really enjoyed attending the church schools in Darfield, especially as I did not have any playmates at Vicar Road as there were few houses. Times were hard for my mother as she only had a widow's pension and there few jobs for women. When I was fourteen I passed an exam which allowed me to attend the new Darfield Senior Selective School. Mum decided to take in lodgers, though we had no bathroom and no electricity. At sixteen I got a job at an ironmonger's shop in Goldthorpe but there was hardly any trade, so found myself on the dole. I kept contacting the Co-op for employment and eventually got a Christmas job, serving toys on the top floor of the Central Store in Barnsley. I then got a permanent job in the underwear section of the Drapery Department. I worked from 8.30 a.m. until 5.30 p.m. with a half day off on a Thursday, but we worked until 9 p.m. on Saturdays. I travelled there on a Camplejohn bus, 8d a day return. I had to wear a hat to go to work and a black dress when serving customers. After a while the manageress sent me and another girl to Kettering for training as a corseteer. When I returned I had to go and visit homes to measure ladies for corsets, travelling all over the Barnsley area, either by bus or on foot. I stayed at the Co-op until 1943 when my son, Martyn, was born.

I first spotted my husband, Fred, when attending church, after I had taken the Sunday school. He was the organ blower. I was a Sunday school teacher from about the age of fifteen. Sometime afterwards I went to a dance at Great Houghton with some friends and we met at the Camplejohns' corner shop (now the museum) and Fred was also waiting there. We became friendly. Eventually, Fred would meet me at the corner shop and we would go walking a lot. We were married at Darfield parish church by Revd Mr Drowns on 1 December 1941. Fred was an RAF clerical worker in Manchester. I had to borrow £5 from my uncle to buy a wedding dress, but we managed to pay it back by the New Year. Our reception at the Reading Room cost £3 and we had a weekend in Blackpool, then Fred had to report back for duty. We couldn't get a house so we lived with my parents in Vicar Road until 1948, Fred returning to his first job, at Houghton Main, where he became a deputy.

Esther wore a dress of white taffeta poult (which she still has), with a Medici collar and orange blossom trimmings. Her plain net veil was surmounted by camellias, and she carried crimson roses and white heather. Mr C. Jones was best man. Among the gifts were a set of carvers from staff at the Barnsley British Co-operative.
Esther Johnson)

Coal miner Willie Marsden (1868–1949) with his wife Sarah Ann (née Ennis, 1872–1945) and grandson William ('Bill') in the backs of their home at Millmoor Terrace, Low Valley, *c.* 1940. Willie worked at Houghton Main and lost an eye in a pit accident. (*Bill Marsden*)

Another generation: William Henry Marsden (1906–92), son of Willie and Sarah shown above, with his son William, *c.* 1939. William was a miner for fifty-one years. (*Bill Marsden*)

William Henry Marsden and his wife, Ella Nora
Wake (b. 1915). The Marsdens were married at
Darfield parish church at 8 a.m. on 4 September
1937, having caught an early no. 70 'Tracky' bus
from Low Valley. They lived at Henry Street.
(*Bill Marsden*)

Third generation of a Low Valley mining
family: William Marsden (b. 1938), joiner
and college lecturer, marries Barbara (née
Lettin), school teacher, 2 August 1969,
Great Houghton Methodist chapel.
(*Bill Marsden*)

An Edwardian wedding party in the grounds of the old rectory at Darfield, *c.* 1910. Miss Bradbury, who wa housekeeper at the rectory, had married the head gardener of Floors Castle, Kelso, so the groom and hi relatives had travelled to Darfield from a considerable distance. Between the bride and groom is Gilber Welford and to the groom's right Mrs Welford. Unusually, all the men are hatless, but each lady wear distinctive though fairly restrained headwear. The bride wears a hat rather than a veil, as was the fashion a this time, and her wedding dress of mixed fabric is possibly cream or pastel in colour. Like the other ladies she is wearing a blouse with a high neckline. The bridesmaids (or at least the ladies with the bouquets) ar wearing matching tailored suits. The groom appears to be wearing a morning suit and a white, high, stiff collared shirt and waistcoat. (*Betty Adams*)

A delightfully informal and working-class wedding group, pictured outside 60 George Street, Low Valley, *c.* 1920. More than fifty friends, neighbours, relatives and a good number of childrer crowd around the bride and groom, William Scargill and Hilda Osborn The Scargills had a fish shop in the area. (*Anna@The Drop Inn*)

ride Hilda Osborne and groom William Scargill, along with
ridesmaids and immediate family. William is sporting a
ashionable trilby hat to accompany his best suit, though the
rousers appear to be a little short. We have a good view of
Hilda's attractive veil and the satin material of the dresses.
Note also the white stockings. The couple may have been
elieved to go inside the house after the photographer had
ompleted his business. The couple's two-tiered wedding cake
 just visible through the window. (*Anna@ The Drop Inn*)

eorge Dickinson (1862–1942) was a popular Darfield
ilkman and postmaster. He also served on the Darfield UDC
or many years. At first he had his own cows, kept by the river,
ut later obtained his milk supplies from Crooke House Farm,
dderthorpe. George's granddaughter, Betty, remembers him
vith great affection and, as a girl, she helped him on his
aturday delivery round. One of the horses that he used was
alled Tommy, a former pit pony. The milk was in two churns
nd ladles were used to dispense the milk. (*Betty Adams*)

Four girls who worked in
Wombwell Co-operative Grocery
shop during the First World
War. Mrs Elsie Weston (née
Small) is second from the left.
(*Zena Hudson*)

Elizabeth Hambleton née
Rodgers (1902–80) enjoys a few
moments with her daughter-in-
law Maureen (1932–94) and
grandson David (b. 1957) at
the 'rec', Low Valley (near
St Barbara's Road). Havelock
Street, now demolished, can be
seen in the background.
(*Malcolm Hambleton*)

8

People, Places
& Occasions

A happy group of children and adults wait in anticipation, perhaps appropriately, at the front of the Prince of Wales public house, Wombwell, flags at the ready, for the royal visit of Queen Elizabeth II and the Duke of Edinburgh, on Wednesday 27 October 1954. The new queen was making a state visit to the West Riding, taking in Barnsley (and what was described in the official programme as 'Mining Areas', plus Wath, Rotherham and Sheffield). They were due to arrive at Wombwell Market Place at 10.50 a.m., to be greeted by the chairman of the council, T.F. Pickering. It was a busy day for the royal party, arriving at Barnsley Exchange station at 10 a.m. and finally leaving Sheffield at 10.50 p.m. (*R.J. Short*)

Residents of Broomhead Road, Wombwell, celebrate the end of the Second World War with a street party. (*Zena Hudson*)

Many Wombwell streets and houses were decked out with flags and bunting to mark the coronation of King George VI, 6 May 1937. This example shows part of Summer Lane/Church Street, near the Alma Inn. (*R.J. Short/M. Robinson*)

Even the smallest of our local communities were keen to celebrate the end of the First World War. At rural Billingley children are pictured at the start of a 'peace tea', the event taking place in Johnson's barn, Manor Farm. Often commemorative mugs were presented to mark such occasions. (*Lynn Bembridge*)

Almost sixty years later residents of Billingley were entertained in a local barn, as part of the queen's Silver Jubilee celebrations, 1977. (*Lynn Bembridge*)

Darfield at War. Residents sign their names on a specially designed petition in support of the Urban District Comforts Fund, on 6 June 1944, D-Day, when Allied forces invaded Normandy. (*Barbara Sanders*)

Two years earlier, in March 1942, a programme was organised in Darfield for Warship Week. Such events took place all over the country in support of the war effort, this one aimed at the funding of warships and weapons. (*Brian Elliott*)

Darfield Warship Week
21st to 28th March, 1942
PROGRAMME

WEDNESDAY, March 25th.
OPEN AFTERNOON, Snape Hill Infants' School, 2.30 p.m.
PHYSICAL TRAINING DISPLAY, Foulstone Modern School, 4.0 to 5.0 p.m., to be followed by First-Aid Party Display.
ALTERATION OF INDICATOR by H. Pickering, Esq., 6.0 p.m.
BILLIARDS EXHIBITION—Mr. H. Townsley (Goldthorpe) versus Local Player. British Legion Club, 7.30 p.m.

THURSDAY, March 26th.
PHYSICAL TRAINING DISPLAY, Foulstone Modern School, 4.0 to 5.0 p.m., to be followed by National Fire Service Display.
NAVAL STORES & PHOTOGRAPHIC EXHIBITION, Foulstone Modern School. To be opened at 4.0 p.m. by Mrs. V. M. Bennett.
ALTERATION OF INDICATOR by L. C. Grocock, Esq., J.P., 6.0 p.m.
CONCERT, Station Hotel, 7.0 p.m.
ONE-ACT PLAYS by Darfield Dramatic Society & League of Youth. Council Schools, Snape Hill Road, 7.0 p.m.

FRIDAY, March 27th.
ALTERATION OF INDICATOR by W. E. Jones, Esq., 6.0 p.m.
CONCERT, Sportsman Inn, 7.0 p.m.
CIVIC BALL, Council School, Snape Hill Road, 9 p.m. to 2 a.m.

SATURDAY, March 28th.
CHINESE ART EXHIBITION, British Legion Club, 3.0 p.m.
ALTERATION OF INDICATOR by A. Brown, Esq., 6.0 p.m.
GRAND CONCERT, British Legion Club, 7.0 p.m.

MONDAY, March 30th.
ALTERATION OF INDICATOR by S. Blackwell, Esq., J.P., 6.0 p.m.

TWO PRIZES OF ONE CERTIFICATE EACH FOR LUCKY PROGRAMME NUMBERS.

Darfield 23rd Company Girl Guides on parade on Church Street, in aid of Hospital Sunday, *c.* 1935. Miss Phyllis Taylor was the guide captain. Those present on the occasion included Esther Johnson and Mabel Woofenden. (*R.J. Short/Esther Johnson*)

The well-equipped Wombwell Salvation Army Band assembles for a commemorative photograph during the miners' strike of 1912. (*Brian Elliott*)

ombwell Operatic Society at the Horse Shoe Hotel, Wombwell. Members of the Operatic Society formed rt of the 'Victorian/Edwardian' audience of *The Good Old Days* at the famous City Varieties, Leeds, in cember 1968. Their VIP invitation came through the close relationship that the society had with the iiseley Operatic Society whose president, Barney Colehan, produced the popular television programme. It is a special day for one of Wombwell's 'cast', Arthur Goldthorpe, who was given the unusual chance of rforming on stage during a gap in filming. This extraordinary event occurred when comedian Johnny ickett 'dried up' and asked for voluntary help. All the society members looked towards Arthur who was a of a joker, so Hackett pulled him out of his seat and on to the stage. Mr Goldthorpe and his wife, Violet, th now in their mid-eighties and married for sixty-five years, have very fond memories of the occasion. eratic Society members, back row, left to right: Tommy Dyson, Eddie Crow, Harry Naylor, -?-, Arthur ldthorpe (wearing straw boater), -?-, -?-, Jack Guest, -?-. Third row: Margaret Turton, Kath Stead, -?-, May chardson, Marie Burrows, -?-, -?-, Edna Sykes, Una Brailsford, -?-, -?-, Sylvia Roberts, Ada Crow. Second w (seated): Gwen Hulley?, Pat Saville, -?-, Maureen Burrows, Nellie Truman, Francie Godridge, Elsie eston, Gerty Taylor, Violet Goldthorpe. Front row: -?-, -?-, -?-, Gordon Truman, Brian Colley, Les Smith, -?-, ctor Stead and Arthur Eastwood. (*Zena Hudson/Sherwood Studios*)

posite, below: There is a long tradition of music, song and drama in and around the Dearne Valley area. embers of the choir of the Hiawatha concert, held at Brampton, respond to a visit from local photographer e Short on 25 January 1947. (*Malcolm Hambleton/R.J. Short*)

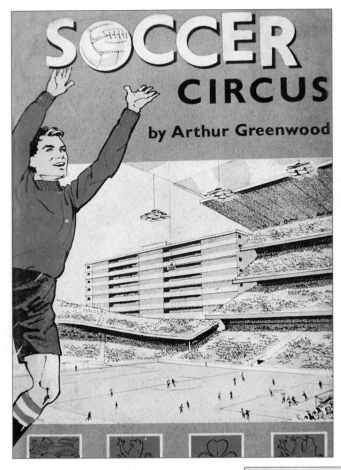

Front cover of *Soccer Circus*, a futuristic novel by Darfield man Arthur Greenwood, published by Macmillan in 1961. A signed copy of the book was presented to each member of the Barnsley Schoolboys football team (including the author, Brian Elliott), just prior to the Yorkshire Shield Quarter Final fixture against York Schoolboys, 13 January 1962. The sliding roof of the stadium featured on the cover pre-dated the one at the new Cardiff Millennium Stadium, a truly remarkable example of Greenwood's amazing foresight and ingenuity. (*Brian Elliott*)

Arthur Greenwood (1903–78), inventor, entrepreneur and novelist, began his working life as an apprentice engineer, and during the Second World War helped in the construction of Howitzer guns. On demob he found himself redundant, so started up his own business manufacturing toys of his own invention, created from drawings produced in his garden shed at Monk Bretton. Moving to Darfield in the 1950s, his Green Monk Products company employed up to 150 people at the School Street factory in Darfield, making a remarkable series of toys such as a Sooty and Sweep xylophone, and exporting to America and Japan. A few years after his death Green Monk Products closed, with the loss of thirty full-time jobs. (*Brian Elliott*)

ne of Arthur Greenwood's Green Monk Products ans, photographed outside the J.C. Snell garage, ew Street, Barnsley, *c.* 1960. Items relating to the terprising and innovative Mr Greenwood can be en on display in the Darfield Heritage Centre and luseum. (*Old Barnsley*)

astles in Spain was performed at the Wombwell mpire, 13–18 February 1950. The cast included uples Muriel and Henry Sykes (left), Wilfred and lna Sykes (centre) and Harry and Madge Crowcroft ight). (*R.J. Short/Terry Sykes*)

South Yorkshire Times

and

Mexborough & Swinton Times.

20 PAGES   FRIDAY, FEBRUARY 18, 1938   140 COLUMNS.

CHILDREN'S TRIBUTE

Ten At Wombwell Veteran's Funeral

The remarkable funeral of John P. Lingard of Station Road, Wombwell was front-page news for the *South Yorkshire Times* on 18 February 1938. John Peacock Lingard, who worked at Houghton Main until he was over seventy years old, was a well-known sports personality. As a young man he trained whippets, some of which became highly successful racing dogs, and was a 'pedestrian' or foot-racer, as was his son, who had trained as a sprinter. Interestingly, he never gambled, despite the preponderance of this activity at sporting events. (*Bill Marsden*)

Programme for the George Street Methodist Sunday School Anniversary, 2 June 1946. the evening performance included a performance of Handel's 'Hallelujah Chorus'. One wonders if the Efficient String Band can be remembered, or the speakers, Mr W. Jinks and J.W. Rowe. (*Bill Marsden*)

George Street Sunday School Prizegiving event, mid-1950s. Among those on the back row are Edna Taylor, Janet Cadwallader, Glennis Upton, Rita Bissell, Sandra Sykes, Joan Cousins, Maxine Haywood, Phyllis Bissell, Jack Shaw, Trevor Palmer, John Pickerill, John Ashwood and Norman Pearson. The middle row includes June Hutchinson, Marilyn Gill, Dorothy Palmer, Lynn Firth, Marcia Dunn, Stuart Cousins and Peter Taylor. The front row of children includes Carol Smallman, Kathryn Cadwallader and Harold Palmer. The teachers, arranged at the front are, left to right, Jim Rowe, William Marsden, Glynnis Walker, Eileen Norton and Janet Cousins. (*Bill Marsden*)

George Street
Methodist Sunday School

LOW VALLEY

ANNIVERSARY

Sunday, 2nd June, 1946

SPEAKERS :

Afternoon at 2-30 : Evening at 6 p.m. :

Mr. W. Jinks, Mr. J. W. Rowe,
Of Wombwell. Of Darfield.

SPECIAL HYMNS AND CHORUSES

will be sung by the Children, Choir and Friends assisted by an Efficient String Band.

Conductor_____Mr. W. SIMMS.
Accompanist_____Mrs. J. PEARSON.
Leader of the Band_____Mr. H. HOLDEN.

COLLECTIONS FOR SUNDAY SCHOOL FUNDS

Thornsby, Printer, Wombwell.

A rare early view of Wombwell's fire engine, a Leyland, with its chief officer and his men ready for action. It was garaged near the brickworks (see the chimney in the background), at the bottom of Station Lane. (*Mr and Mrs D. Camplejohn*)

A tram (car no. 17), bound for Thurnscoe, makes its way along High Street, Wombwell, in this fine Scrivens postcard, *c. 1925*. The service, operated by the Dearne District Light Railway Committee, started on 14 July 1924, but proved to be a financial disaster, closing at the end of September 1933. (*Old Barnsley*)

In the days before holidays were taken on a more regular basis, local beauty spots were popular with courting couples. The early postcard makers were not slow to capitalise on this fact of everyday life, in this example producing a 'Lovers Walk' image which could be conveniently stamped on the front to localise the scene. A great deal of artistic licence was obviously shown in term of people density and the agility of tree-climbing couples! This particular card was posted in Wombwell on 15 September 1906, with the tongue-in-cheek comment, 'How will this do for Wombwell Wood'. (*Brian Elliott*)

Numerous 'real photograph' topographical cards were also published, featuring Wombwell Wood. This interesting example (card no. 1 of a series) shows a small group of very well-dressed Edwardian ladies resting by an avenue of beech trees. Unfortunately there is no sign of any courting couples, despite the presence of sturdy branches, though a fair bit of graffiti is visible on the tree trunks, one engraving left by 'S.H.' in 1894. (*Brian Elliott*)

A wonderful Edwardian view of the Darfield Bridge area. The shopkeeper in his apron may be George
Jackson from the corner shop at the bottom of Pinfold Lane, and we also have a good glimpse of the late
medieval Bridge Inn, kept by the Noble family. (*Malcolm Hambleton*)

The 'propped up' Bridge Inn as it appeared in the late 1960s, not long before its unfortunate demolition. It
still retained its old sign, over the left-hand doorway. The more modern sign advertised the Oakwell Ales of
the Barnsley Brewery Co. (*Bill Marsden*)

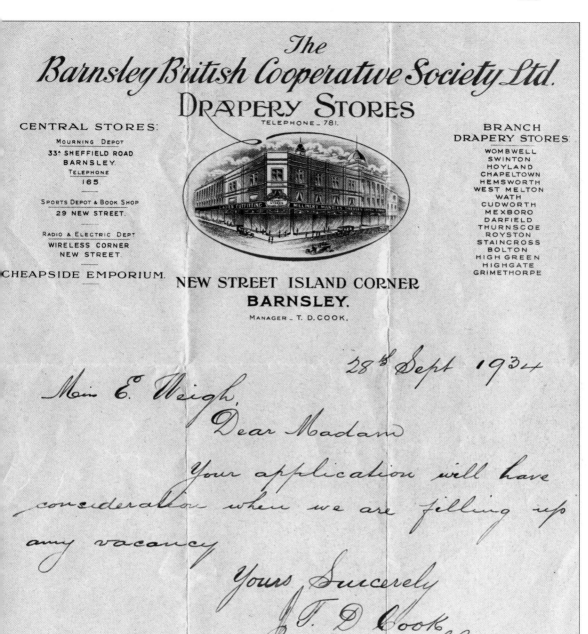

The
Barnsley British Cooperative Society Ltd.
DRAPERY STORES
TELEPHONE - 781.

CENTRAL STORES:

MOURNING DEPOT
33ᴬ SHEFFIELD ROAD
BARNSLEY.
TELEPHONE
165

SPORTS DEPOT & BOOK SHOP
29 NEW STREET.

RADIO & ELECTRIC DEPT
WIRELESS CORNER
NEW STREET.

CHEAPSIDE EMPORIUM.

BRANCH
DRAPERY STORES

WOMBWELL
SWINTON
HOYLAND
CHAPELTOWN
HEMSWORTH
WEST MELTON
WATH
CUDWORTH
MEXBORO
DARFIELD
THURNSCOE
ROYSTON
STAINCROSS
BOLTON
HIGH GREEN
HIGHGATE
GRIMETHORPE

NEW STREET ISLAND CORNER
BARNSLEY.
MANAGER - T. D. COOK.

28ᵗʰ Sept 1934

Miss E. Weigh,

Dear Madam

Your application will have consideration when we are filling up any vacancy

Yours Sincerely
T. D. Cook
GK

letter signed on the behalf of T.D. Cook, Manager of the Barnsley British Co-operative Society Drapery
ores Ltd, to Miss Esther Weigh of Darfield, acknowledging her job application, dated 28 September 1934.
ote the impressive letterhead, featuring New Street Island Corner, one of the showpiece stores of the
ompany. (*Esther Johnson*)

The view from Darfield church tower, probably on a Saturday in the 1950s, shows children leaving the Darfield Empire cinema after a matinee performance. (*Brian Elliott*)

Front cover of a postwar Darfield Empire cinema programme for June 1948, when you could enjoy a couple of films, buy refreshments and a programme, and still have change from half a crown! (*Barbara Sanders*)

DARFIELD
EMPIRE

Telephone: Wombwell 205
Proprietor — R. T. REDMAYNE.

**Programme for
JUNE, 1948**

PRICE ½d EACH

Programme Subject to Alteration

**ONCE NIGHTLY AT 6-30
SATURDAY 6.0 & 8.15**

**BALCONY 1/6
AREA 9d. & 5d.**
INCLUDING TAX